DOUBLE EXIT

DOUBLE EXIT

When Aging Couples
Commit Suicide Together

Ann Wickett

Double Exit

A paperback original

First published, 1989,
by the Hemlock Society
PO Box 11830
Eugene OR 97440
U S A

Library of Congress number: HV6546.W53   1989

ISBN number : 0–9606030–7–7

In Memory of Paula Caucanas-Pisier

How I begrudge the body's slow death;
would rather be seized and eaten
by an eagle or a sharp fish
than by this inward worming.

Must we live at last in a house with dirty windows
and doors that will not open,
the chimneys clogged and the hearthfire grown too sluggish
to make real flames anymore?

To desire nothing anymore
except sleep?

If only one could
spin some kind of cocoon
and then wait mindless
as a caterpillar that winters on a bare branch.

—Peggy Pond Church
1904–1986

Contents

Preface

Ann Wickett now adds to our understanding of human life and death, both in the
way of perception and in knowledge. In the last
quarter of a century we have had a remark-
ably swift change in attitudes toward dying.
The conventional wisdom has matured a lot
and ancient taboos have surrendered to more
rational behavior.

Perhaps this surge of choice and human
initiatives in dying is part of the modern new
spirit of personal liberty and respect for human rights—a spirit seen not only in birth
control and death control but in the levelling
of man-woman relations, in equality of racial
and minority status, freedom to travel and
learn, and a growing concern with the quality of life.

The old hopeless submission to a "sanc-
tity of life" doctrine had—since the classical
Greek and Roman outlook was squashed in
the Western world—denied all personal
rights in dealing with dying.

The cases in this book are a treasure, and great credit goes to the author for finding them and collecting them together. It is often said that a picture is worth a hundred pages, and it seems to me a real case is worth a hundred pages of abstract philosophy. Real cases stir up the imagination, and, as the physicist Albert Einstein put it, imagination is more important than knowledge.

The essence of euthanasia is the right to choose to die rather than suffer maladies which are no longer reversible. Champions of euthanasia, of which Ann Wickett and her husband Derek Humphry are two of the staunchest, have given us all a lesson in how to change the world in spite of its often deep mire in prejudice. Bernard Shaw was correct when he said a reasonable person adapts to the status quo while an unreasonable person persists in trying to adapt the world to himself; therefore all progress depends on unreasonable people.

I have myself been a part of the growing forces of euthanasia, pleading the case for the right to choose to die by Living Wills and other legal supports, and for assistance to those who choose to die in hopeless circumstance—especially expert medical help—and here in this book we have a fresh kind of document, and a very welcome one.

There is good reason to suspect that the actual effect of prefaces is only to postpone the feast books lay before us. The hint of truth in this thought leads me, then, to stop this preface.

Joseph Fletcher

Charlottesville, Virginia
Summer, 1988

Acknowledgments

Special thanks go to Marion Freeman, Bob Tinnon, and Michael White for their input and encouragement. Any errors or omissions are my responsibility. Needless to say, everyone who contributed their stories to this book deserves a special vote of thanks, even though they shall remain nameless. I am especially grateful to my husband, Derek Humphry, whose idea it was for me to write this book. Not only was he endlessly supportive, he was a stalwart in helping with the typing and editing of the manuscript.

Introduction

Two years ago, my parents died. They died together, and they died intentionally.

After bidding goodbye to close family members, they took an overdose of barbiturates with several ounces of alcohol. When their bodies were found, they looked as if they were dozing peacefully. I never forgot that.

My father was 92, my mother 78. Both had been plagued with grave illnesses for years, and the prognosis was dim. Nursing homes, increasing paralysis, and the loss of their home were all they had to look forward to—well-meaning but alien health-care workers invading their privacy, medical teams insisting on resuscitation against my parents' will, and a spiraling loss of control.

Finally, as my father explained, he and my mother had had enough. There was nowhere else they wanted to go, nothing else they wanted to do. There was nothing more they *could* do, he added, except look forward to further suffering, dependence, and helplessness. They had had enough of life, and what remained promised to be painful and remorseless. It was time to say goodbye.

He and my mother said this to me one hot and humid summer evening. Two weeks later they were dead.

The manner of their deaths made an extraordinary impression on me, no less so because the marriage had been far from ideal. It surprised me that they had become so united and that they were able to take so forceful a step. They were unassuming, compliant people. Yet their final years—a dying by millimeters, my father called it—became intolerable for them. Affronted and humiliated by the growing indignities of their deterioration, they decided to do something about it.

After they died, and after sorting through all my feelings, I realized that, more than anything, I was proud of what they had done. I wish things had been better for them during their final years, but, in the end, my father and mother countered their growing helplessness with an action that had the abandon of youth and the flavor of true existentialism. Not only would they take charge of their living, they would take charge of their dying.

It's time for us to say farewell, my mother and father said that hot summer night.

And they did.

What had influenced their decision-making?

Although both my grandfathers died quickly and relatively painlessly, my mother's mother lingered in nursing homes for years, desperate to die but condemned to life because she had a strong heart. I remember visiting her in one nursing home; I was not more than ten years old. I went up three flight of stairs and got lost in a labyrinth of gloomy corridors before finding her room at the end of the hall. It was hot and humid and there were no fans. I opened her door and saw her sitting in a tiny, spartan room, staring out the window. The walls were painted men's lavatory green. There was brown linoleum on the floor, a single cot, a dingy chest of drawers and little else.

As young as I was, I knew it was degrading for a woman of my grandmother's stature, someone who had been kind and outgoing, to have to end her life in a cell. I stared at the back of her head for a long time. She was deaf and could not hear me. She just continued to stare out the window at nothing. I think, even at ten years of age, I could feel her heart breaking.

Inevitably her health worsened, and she was transferred to another nursing home where she was bedridden, spoonfed, and occasionally diapered. My parents' visits became less and less frequent. Finally, when my mother came back one afternoon to tell me that my grandmother had died, I was relieved but was too ashamed to say it aloud. Perhaps my mother was relieved, too. I don't recall that she cried.

Now that I am older, I think a lot about this woman who must have wondered what she had done to deserve the decade of suffering before she finally died.

My other grandmother, my father's mother, was passed from one relative to another after her husband died. In family conferences, the words duty and obligation were mentioned a great deal. Grandma was sent from one son to another to another daughter. We dreaded it when it was our turn, and there were angry words between my parents about others not assuming their "share of the burden." And that is exactly what my grandmother had become: a burden—an unwanted, barely tolerated inconvenience. Or, as my mother rather unceremoniously put it, "A pain in the neck."

The rotation went on for several years. My grandmother had an extraordinary capacity for staying alive, which irritated everyone. "The food bill!" my mother would say over and over again, even though Grandma ate like a sparrow. My father and his brother and sister bickered over time-shares and contributions as if their mother were an unwanted commodity. I cannot remember her death. She was simply rotated one more time and never came back.

It was shortly after this that I first heard my parents express their determination never to become such burdens. "Not like *them*," they would repeat over and over, saying it with such vehemence that it startled me. They were my mother and father, and I could not imagine them being anything other than what they were supposed to be—two people who were put on earth to look after me indefinitely. I was still too young to imagine that it could happen to us all. Old age. Reduced finances. Helplessness. Loss of pride. Desperation. Fear. My father's mother staring vacuously at banal television programs for hours at a stretch was, I realize now, no less heart-rendering than my mother's mother staring wordlessly out a window with no view. Nothing made sense to them any more.

This, then, was my parents' legacy. As they grew older and sicker, whatever extended family remained had a disruptive, menacing influence. One sister, my father's, died on welfare. His only brother committed suicide in 1973 after a series of illnesses which led to chronic depression. My mother's sister was mentally and physically unwell, exhaustingly tended by a husband who had become a full-time caretaker. Surveying the rest of the family, my parents must have guessed that what lay ahead of them.

It took me a while to put the pieces together, but finally I began to understand. Family assistance, a dubious blessing, had been replaced with something even worse: institutionalization.

In 1980, my husband, Derek Humphry, and I founded the Hemlock Society, a non-profit educational organization that advo-

5

cates the right of a terminally ill patient to accelerate the dying process, if he chooses, through the aid of a physician. My husband was motivated by his experience with his previous wife, who suffered from cancer for two and a half years before dying. Finally, when she was close to the end, he helped her take an overdose as she had requested; she did not want to die in a hospital, nor did she want to die in a vegetative state.

We wrote about this in *Jean's Way*, which, without our intending, propelled us in the direction of the euthanasia movement. Because there was such a demand for more acceptable alternatives for the dying and so few available, we were increasingly asked to devise a plan which would include both passive and active voluntary euthanasia options for the terminally ill. Finally, after respective careers in journalism and academia, Derek and I formed Hemlock, hoping, first, to increase public awareness about the needs of the dying, and, second, to draft legislation which would codify physician aid-in-dying.

I have often wondered why I ended up working in this field. When Derek and I wrote *Jean's Way*, I was hardly aware of the meaning of the word euthanasia. Yet when I think of my parents, I was probably influenced at a very early age. I remember being terribly impressed every time my father would say (not without some humor) that he would never let old age undo him; he hoped a huge boulder would fall on him first. Although I was young, I knew he meant it. I think that as many as 30 years before he died, he had his end planned.

Thus, when Derek and I told him about Jean's death and the subsequent formation of Hemlock, he nodded knowingly. He and my mother became our first members. She sent newspaper cuttings of cases where people were kept alive on life-supports against their will, with notes expressing her horror. They both sent annual donations with compliments about the growth of the Society and its goals.

Considering this, perhaps my involvement in the right-to-die movement is not entirely by chance. And considering the impact my parents' death had on me, the nature of this book is not surprising either.

Research for this book, prompted by my parents' deaths, was carried out primarily by me and two researchers. To get a more comprehensive view of simultaneous deaths (as they are called) over the last seven decades, interviews and correspondence with surviving family members provided invaluable firsthand information.

Also, Hemlock researchers Susan Waller and Joyce Rotheram spent six months in the archives of the University of Southern California and UCLA libraries, with access to the national Bureau for Health Statistics.

Eventually, a substantial file on all euthanasia-related cases emerged, containing every documented instance of death hastened by assistance, whether by health-care worker, relative, or friend since 1920. (Not only were records prior to 1920 poorly documented, remarkable advances in medical technology were just beginning to alter dramatically treatment of patients by then; many were now having their lives prolonged, despite painful and long-suffering terminal illnesses.)

The Hemlock file also contained a growing number—meager at first, but steadily increasing—of the curious phenomenon of double suicides and mercy-killings/suicides.

However, as exhaustive as these techniques were, one still has to allow for the number of cases that went unreported or simply slipped through the cracks. Although almost all mercy-killings/suicides have been consistently reported in the last 65 years since they involve felonious behavior, statistics on double suicides must be considered conservative estimates. Too often authorities are willing to turn a blind eye to the manner of death out of respect for the surviving family members. Also, figures are too small to be considered statistically significant, even though definite trends can be discerned, trends which are a disturbing portent for future decades.

This book is an attempt to trace these patterns in the growing phenomenon of couples who intentionally die together. In identifying these factors, an attempt has been made to pinpoint the tragic circumstances surrounding such deaths. All information gathered is part of an argument for change:

While suicide remains an inalienable right, it should not be a desperate, last resort when all else fails and when there are no better options available.

Above all, the old and sick should be regarded as valuable and worthwhile people, not discards. For them, there must be better, more humane alternatives than overdosing, gassing, or shooting themselves to death.

They deserve more.

Ann Wickett

Eugene, Oregon
September, 1988

I.

Double Suicide:
A First-Hand Account

After my parents' deaths, I wrote several articles about double suicide either by drug overdose or by carbon monoxide poisoning. I also wrote about mercy-killings/suicides, where one spouse kills another, usually with a gun, and then kills him or herself. I was curious to see if there were other people out there willing to talk about what is technically called the simultaneous death of two married people. Statistics show that what happened to my parents isn't so unusual: Not only is the suicide rate of the elderly skyrocketing, the rate of mercy-killings/suicides and double suicides among old, ailing couples in the 1980s is literally going off the charts.

Whatever response I got from family members indicated that, despite the trauma, there was often sympathy and compassion over what had happened. In other instances, understanding came late and with hindsight. Yet regardless of the circumstances, sons and daughters expressed sorrow that their parents had not had better alternatives, horror when there had been bloodshed, and guilt if there had been distance and erratic communication between them, which was frequently the case.

When parents had communicated their intentions to grown children, sons and daughters suffered the agony of trying to respect the decision while being torn over the impending loss of both mother and father. Quite a few parents relied on a son or daughter (sometimes both) for permission and final approval of their suicides. This was a heavy burden indeed. "I was, in effect, sanctioning my parents' deaths," one man commented. "It was so unnatural at first, I felt as if I was breaking some kind of taboo. Maybe I was."

On balance, when two elderly people decide to end their lives, it is difficult enough if the family has lived together harmoniously and communication has been open. Yet in reality, such "perfect" families rarely exist. More commonly old, unhealthy patterns remain: Unresolved disputes, favoritism—real or imagined, subtle scapegoating, and long-standing grievances linger. The added stress of having to deal with aging parents can also have an exhausting effect on family members who, aside from whatever differences remain, now have to confront one another with life-and-death decisions. For those who are incapable of putting aside their differences, there is little chance that old scores will be settled and that the best kind of decision-making occur.

As seen in the following account, told to this writer, Claudia Lugus (not her real name) chronicles the ways in which the strains of aging, illness, and isolation have a chaotic and disruptive effect on the immediate family. Some members cope better than others. One sister, Susan, retreated from the demands of caring for her parents, despite the fact she had lived with them nearly all her life. This left Claudia, after years of estrangement, as an ad hoc caretaker when her parents made it clear they had no one else to turn to.

Poor communication among family members added to the confusion. Ironically, Claudia found herself increasingly responsible as she and her parents realized that physicians and health-care workers, although well-meaning, were limited in caring for the very old and very ill. Others, such as neighbors, withdrew, feeling that they could be of no real help.

Typically, as in most such stories, there is no villain. Aging and becoming ill are realities that takes their toll. If the quest is to grow old and accept death with dignity, Claudia Lugus's account leaves one wondering: How?

It is a Thursday when he calls. Late Thursday afternoon.

I can remember the exact time and date because my stitches have just been removed. I have had cosmetic surgery on my eyes, corrective surgery on the lower eye lids. The telephone rings as I study the scar tissue on my lower eyelids. I say hello, the receiver in one hand, a mirror in the other.

It is my father. I cannot remember the last time I had heard from him. There is stilted, cursory small talk—the weather, my husband, our health. I know this is not the real reason he is calling.

Finally, after a deep breath: You've got to help us, he says. Pause. Your mother and I can't go on like this. Another pause.

He speaks crustily, a tone I recognize as embarrassment when he has to confront unpleasant truths. Like my mother, my father has let much of life happen to him, at least in the later years. Now, despite infrequent phone calls and practically no letters, I know that a series of debilitating illnesses is nudging them toward the grave. Dying is happening to them. They can't pretend otherwise.

It is a curious juxtaposition for me, this telephone call and my new eyes. I have just returned from a clinic where moribund skin cells are camouflaged, revitalized, and re-suscitated. In the midst of bobbed noses and taut cheekbones, one's mortality is defied by an endlessly cheery medical staff in Reebok running shoes. I can cheat aging a bit, everyone there can cheat aging a bit, but for my parents the reality is inescapable.

My father's voice continues: We don't know what will happen, where to go, he says, taking a deep breath. I visualize him sitting by the telephone, staring at the floor.

I put the mirror down and wait. There is silence at the other end. Then I say: Tell me how I can help you.

My relationship with my parents has never been an easy one. Thus, the phone call presents me with another curious juxtaposition: My father has appealed to me with an intimacy that is incredible considering the difficult nature of our relationship. Over the years, periods of communication, never very good, have been punctuated by periods of estrangement. In the last two years I have made more of an effort. Two years earlier my mother, 79, suffered a stroke. Already afflicted with arthritis, this was a real blow. My father, then over 80, became her principal caretaker.

My parents are utterly isolated even though my sister, Susan, and her son live nearby. I have sensed from earlier conversations with my parents that whatever visits they have had from their grandson and Susan are infrequent and distressing. I use that phrase as I try to describe to Hank, my husband, what's happening. Distressing. Without substance. Fitful.

He reminds me of my sister's sole communication with us several months earlier.

We have not spoken in 19 years, yet one afternoon she did telephone, leaving a brief, distressing message with Hank; she seemed reluctant to talk to me. I can't take any more, she told him. I'm washing my hands of them, she added, hanging up quickly. When I tried to call her back, there was no answer.

I leave it, but I can't forget what she has said.

On Thursday my conversation with my father is longer than usual. Later I wonder if it is the medication I am taking for my eyes that makes me less reserved, more approachable. How bad is it? I say, not wanting to hear his answer.

He reels off a series of disasters that leaves me, for the moment, speechless. One: My mother falls in the shower, cutting her head open. Another: My mother and father fall together, neither of them able to get up. My father crawls to the telephone to call for a neighbor's help. Another: My mother falls again, hitting her head on the radiator. This time she refuses to be treated. She and my father sit and wait for Lech, the Polish man who acts as a kind of aged houseboy for my parents, coming a few hours six days a week. When he finally arrives, my parents are sitting at the dining room table, my mother holding a towel drenched in blood.

I'm sorry, I say, interrupting my father. I want him to stop telling me these things. I don't want to live with the images he has forced on me.

It's gone on too long, he says. Another pause. There are many of them, many sighs. Then: Why go on living like this? We don't want to.

Now it's my turn to pause. I'll fly over there in two weeks, I finally say, calculating how I can fit a visit into my schedule. It has been nearly 24 months since I have seen them. Almost as an afterthought, I add, Have you stockpiled drugs? Would you ever have enough?

I am amazed at my boldness. My father says he's not sure, and as we say goodbye, he asks if he may send me a list of the drugs he does have. Would you examine and research the inventory? he asks, actually using that word, *inventory*. Yes, I answer, even further amazed. We speak as if we were discussing real estate or municipal bonds.

We hang up.

My husband, a writer for documentary films, has been researching a story about handicapped people. Overworked and distracted by problems of his own, Hank has asked me to interview a quadriplegic man paralyzed by a multiple car crash: All he can move are a few fingers of one hand. A friend has devised an electronic alphabet board so he can communicate simple commands. Hank thinks the story might be worth pursuing.

It is this visit I have in mind while figuring out the best way to see my parents. Their home is only a short plane ride from the quadriplegic. I have agreed to do the interview for Hank and have just made plane reservations. It occurs to me that I would not have considered seeing my parents if my father had not requested it.

Discussing the trip to my parents', my husband and I talk about the implications of what my father has told me. Hank expresses no shock or surprise. In our 8-year marriage, he has developed a long-distance affection for my father, a gentle tolerance for my mother. He urges me to stay with my parents as long as I wish. We agree, however, that two weeks is probably enough.

Four days later the letter from my father arrives. In his shaky but determined hand, on legal lined paper to facilitate the ever-present carbon copy, he confirms my visiting dates and time of arrival. Looking forward to your being here, he writes at the top of the page. My father is a polite man. He then gets to the heart of the matter.

Now about the medication. I have been taking .25 mg of digoxin each day for 3–5 years for my congestive heart condition. Might 40–80 ensure lethality? Together with any immunity factor and the possibility of nausea and vomiting, this seems uncertain to say the least.

Sleeping pills. Shortly after Mother's stroke, I took at bedtime 1 Meprobamate (400 mg.). After 6 months or so, Dr. Rosenthal changed to Restoril (15 mg.), but I am now going back to Meprobamate as Restoril seems less effective. Dr. R. says Meprobamate are stronger than Seconal. Can you verify this?

I have another sleeping potion in liquid form—Noctec. Dosage is one half teaspoon (250 mg.) at bedtime. Have not used it yet except once. It tasted awful.

Of course, I have considered auto exhaust. However, I am a little forgetful and weak physically, so there is a risk that, if not successful, I would get some sort of impairment and be worse off.

The next paragraph stuns me. Since my birth, my father and I have rarely dared be candid with one another. He, a shy, complex man, and I, a defensive, remote daughter, are now negotiating life-and-death matters. He writes:

I see absolutely no chance of getting the right kind of Seconal-Codeine combination that would assure lethality. Is there a chance that you could get them—I realize this is an imposition—but I wondered if you knew a drug supplier? You can imagine the response from Dr. Konig (a neighbor) and Dr. Rosenthal.

He mentions how difficult the letter has been to write and closes by referring to family plans with characteristic propriety: Of course, I would not do anything until after Ted's (a grand-nephew) wedding on March 5, he writes. He thanks me for my interest, sends his love, and signs the letter Dad.

I hold the letter for a long time. I then show it to my husband. Go to the library, he says. We don't know any drug suppliers.

I can hardly believe what's happening and spend the rest of the day reading and re-reading the letter. It is impossible to absorb all that my father is telling me. Death is not something that requires family planning, I think. Or is it? The urgency in my father's voice, the images he has thrust on me, are things I can't let go of, no matter how hard I try.

Very well. I convince myself that I am doing research. Something else will turn up, some miracle of health-care that will make things better for them. In the mean-time, he needs me. That is something both unusual and deeply moving. I know it has not been easy for him to ask for help, especially from me.

I cancel a lunch the following day and do my research. I can't cry but I want to. I also feel curiously galvanized. I'm not sure why.

My father was born near the turn of the century when Henry Ford built his first car, a curious contraption like a four-wheel bicycle with a forward rudder for steering. Clearly, the industrial revolution was in full swing, good news for my father's father, Carl, who, with his only brother, was a foundryman. Their father had been a milkman, a Scandanavian immigrant who kept two Percheron mares and had a reputation as the best draft-horse driver in the county.

My grandmother's name was Rosie Murphy, although photographs show a woman who looks anything but cheerful. Rosie's features are too broad for her head and she pouts nonstop, as if the expression had been chiselled on her face at birth. One of thirteen children, the daughter of a New York policeman who was retired early for heavy drinking, Rosie married Carl when she was in her late teens and he in his early twenties. They settled in a two-story, two-family stucco house in a working-class suburb of Chicago, where they raised three sons, my father the eldest, and two daughters. The house is unbearably drab but immaculate.

In contrast to Rosie, Carl was handsome and good-natured. His even, patrician features blended with his wife's broader ones to produce a sensuous, earnest, not unattractive combination in their children. The mouth is full, the eyes guarded but intense. The word no-nonsense comes to mind in the appearance of everyone in the family except my grandfather, who always looked wistful.

After my father graduated from high school, there was a doggedness suggesting a vision of sorts: He set about singlehandedly educating his brothers and sisters. After attending university for a year, he transferred to night school. Days, he worked as a bookkeeper, sending one sister to nursing school and another to secretarial college.

After graduating from night school, he joined the army and during this time he managed to save enough money to send one younger brother, Peter, to Yale University. Yale! When my father went back to his accounting career, he paid for three more years at business school for Peter. (He also sent his youngest brother to Northwestern during this time.) Graduation pictures at Yale show Peter soberly clutching his diploma. Rosie stands erect and impassive in a shapeless black dress. Typically, Carl looks sweet, handsome, and overawed.

My father is there too, still handsome and solemn, but looking reticent and virginal too. Perhaps this was why he would remain unmarried for years. For some reason, when I study this picture, the word law-abiding comes to mind. Maybe this is what drove him, what he inherited from his unfrivolous mother and submissive father: Obey the rules, don't overindulge, mind your manners, God is vengeful.

I look at this final picture of him as a young man (there is a notable absence of photographs until his marriage years later), and I sense someone who cannot properly fuse his mother's rigidity with his father's wistfulness. He is frozen in the photograph, my father, but one senses that the same quality accompanied him outside the critical eye of the camera, as if parts of him had been ossified at a precise moment in his life and remained that way.

What surfaced was a son, my father, whose good-naturedness was a dull concession to both parents, a middle-of-the-road compromise that dared not veer into any extreme—passion, willfulness, submission, or fantasy.

Instead, he plodded on, gazing neither too far to the left nor to the right. My father became a kind of Dobbin.

By the time he met my mother, he had moved to Philadelphia, where he had graduated to a senior executive position for a bottling firm and drove a crimson, four-door Packard. My mother was his secretary. While my father was tall and solid, she was diminutive. They were opposites in many ways.

The daughter of two school teachers, my mother was reared in modest gentility. Her father, Esmond, the son of a prosperous merchant, attended seminary and later graduate school in the classics. Before graduating in 1903, he posed for a photograph in his study: Erect in a ladder-back chair, he rests his head against a pale hand, his pince-nez poised on an aquiline nose, his desk filled with leather-clad volumes. He is already balding.

At 25, he married my grandmother, the same age. The daughter of a bank manager, Luella was an elementary school teacher when she met her future husband. Not a beauty, her face could be described as moony but intelligent. She too wore pince-nez.

Within two years of their marriage she became pregnant with the first of their two children, Henry. My mother was born four years later and turned out to be the somber beauty of the family, an aristocratic-looking young woman with wonderful ankles, breasts, and waistline. She was formally photographed in satin dresses, yet there is a staged, contrived aspect to her appearance, as if she had wandered into the wrong room in an ill-fitting costume. Henry, her brother, simply stands and endures the camera as if he had abandoned hope long ago.

Both children dutifully took violin and piano lessons and helped organize church teas. Later, they attended the local university. After graduation, Henry married a librarian and spent the rest of his life as a law clerk. It was a plodding, unsuccessful career and marriage, with no children and intermittent bouts of depression, which no one was able to explain.

My mother, on the other hand, as a kind of fluke, accepted a position with the bottling firm in Philadelphia where my father worked. Later she would tell me that it was an attempt to escape from a life she had found suffocating. Whatever the case, at some point, her relationship with my father became social; he occasionally took her to dinner and the theatre where, as she related years later, he fell asleep. After a year he proposed marriage and she accepted.

There are no letters or photographs from their engagement period. Nor are there any of their marriage in Philadelphia. I can never remember them referring to this period at all, except that it "happened."

After settling into married life, my parents fell into a routine and, inevitably, a decline. When Susan was born, the birth was considered something to celebrate. Two years later, there was a son who died shortly after birth. Maybe this was the turning point. Whatever the case, by the time I appeared, the marriage had unravelled in ways that would never be repaired. As my mother was to say later, things just "fell apart." She never said why. Apparently they never got better.

As it was, there is only one picture of my mother and me. She is sitting in a garden chair, with Susan on her lap, and me—about one and a half—leaning on the chair's arm. I am rather tenuously balanced with my hands waving riotously. My mother has one arm in back of Susan, the other draped carelessly behind me, not, apparently, touching either of us.

She looks away from the camera, sitting placidly in a summer dress. At first, there doesn't appear to be anything wrong until one notices a missing button on her dress and runs in her stockings. Her eyes, though open, are distant and unfocused. The picture seems to say: I am here, but I am not here. That's your mother? a friend asked me. I thought it was a stranger.

But that's the way she was, I say. Looking into her eyes was like looking into an aquarium.

I remember all this vividly as I make plans to return to Philadelphia, to the same rambling, slightly dishevelled brick colonial that my parents bought before I was born. My mother and father want to die, and I am flooded with memories of the way they used to be when they were younger and larger than life in my eyes. I need to know who they were in order to say goodbye, if that is possible.

In the meantime, Hank and I plan my trip. I have gone to the library and culled enough information from pharmacy text-books to get a good idea of the lethal doses of some of my father's drugs. It's all there, if one looks hard enough: cold, bone-chilling facts about toxicity, lethalness, and coma-inducing doses. Coma-inducing! Occasionally I look up from the weighty volumes at the studious people around me, clean-cut, earnest faces peering at books about Jane Austin, beaver dams, and the gross national product. And there I sit, writing down information about how many pills it will take to kill my parents.

Still, I convince myself that this is an exercise. A research project. I have to convince myself of this because as helpful as the information might be, there are so many other variables, things which I can't begin to guess at or want to: drug tolerance, body weight, and accessibility, let alone the fact that my father plans to use whatever information I send him to do himself in. And of course my biggest worry is that an overdose will not be enough; as my father said in his letter, he'll be even worse off than before. Won't I be the one to blame?

During the week before I leave, I have many dreams, reminiscent and distressing. The one that repeats itself is about a book my father gave me when I was a child. Inside was a picture of a lamb with a real bell attached. In the dream I am afraid to tell my father I don't like the book (which is curious; I loved it) for fear he will be upset. Yet in my dream I tell him I am unhappy with it.

He gazes at me and then puts his head in his hands, crying uncontrollably. He cannot stop. My mother looks on impassively.

Finally, it's time to leave. Hank and I have spent the week planning my trip with a detachment that's chilling, but I let it go. I know that a part of me cannot believe what is happening, just as a part of Hank is incredulous too. He has treated the whole thing with a bemused detachment, the kind he uses for projects that are well-meaning but which he knows will never materialize.

It's probably wishful thinking on both our parts; I know that I am participating in some absurd exercise, that I will step off the plane and walk through the front door of my parents' house and be greeted by two middle-aged people who are mowing the lawn and preparing dinner and complaining about the price of rib roast. They will criticize my clothes and my hair, as they always have. They don't suit you, they will say almost in unison.

But, no, now it is I who am middle-aged, who mows the lawn and has eyes reshaped by cosmetic surgeons and wears a hairstyle and clothes that are conservative, even by my parents' standards. Yet no matter how hard I try, I cannot shake off past perceptions and deal with present ones—decrepit, aging, frightened parents. I retreat into an automaton state in which I see myself as a cross between geriatric counsellor and pharmaceutical adviser.

Or, in darker moments, compassionate executioner.

I never mention this to Hank. It is a difficult time for him. Only weeks earlier, his eldest son, Will, from his first marriage, was arrested for drunk driving. Several people were injured. We know the penalty will be heavy. He helps me pack in an absent-minded fashion and we chat desultorily about the weather, avoiding the topics that really concern us. We drink some wine and I close and lock the one suitcase I am taking with me.

I am travelling unusually light. Aside from a pair of cashmere trousers, I am taking nothing glamorous. This is uncharacteristic. I invariably use travel as an excuse to dress up, brighten up. Now I am dressing down, the colors of my wardrobe earth tones, muted, hesitant statements about my visibility.

Tucked in between my hot curlers and a bottle of Scotch is what we call our "research paper," as well as an extraordinary piece of information Hank has obtained. He stumbled on it in the midst of an interview, and passed it on to me without much comment. Through one of the handicapped people Hank has been interviewing, a certain barbiturate, unavailable in America, can be ordered through a pharmacy in Europe: The caller presents himself as a physician and asks that the prescription be charged to his or her Visa account. Incredible!

Without much comment on my part—the plot of this is becoming rapidly astonishing—I pocket the information with two names and numbers. One is that of a psychologist suffering from multiple sclerosis. Another is that of the European pharmacy which takes orders in English. It was the psychologist who discovered the European source (her brother is a doctor) and has ordered sufficient quantities, as she told Hank, so that she doesn't die slowly and painfully. The name of the barbiturate is Vesparax, and 20 are lethal.

Hank and I agree that it should be up to my parents to make contact with either the psychologist or the European pharmacy, but I know that neither of us really thinks this will happen. It has to be their decision, he says at the airport, but he says it in such a way that suggests an entirely hypothetical scenario. I nod and we embrace. He is concerned but distracted, and I feel as if we are losing each other.

As I board the plane, I remember a letter my mother wrote me years earlier; I was single and pregnant and asked my parents for help. You're killing your father, she wrote.

I consider the irony of this statement, something I will spend more time thinking about in the weeks ahead. Can my parents and I ever smooth over the rough and distressing edges of the past? Is all this talk about death simply an excuse to heal old wounds? There are many of them. Maybe too many.

I fasten my seatbelt and take a deep breath. Who knows.

I have no idea where my mother stands in all this. Throughout my childhood, she was a distant, brooding figure, given to hand-wringing and stacatto gestures with her body. I can never remember her physically touching me or saying anything that meant anything.

I was, however, aware of an enduring sadness in her, of long and silent lunches as she sat at a far end of the kitchen eating a tasteless sandwich. What's wrong, I would ask, and she would sigh and shrug and stare out the window. She dressed in greys and browns and wore skirts and blouses that didn't match. She had given up wearing make-up and let her hair grow long and shapeless.

I remember a lot about her on my flight back to Philadelphia, not all of it things I want to remember. The excrement on the kitchen floor one morning. I couldn't make it to the bathroom in time, she said to me as she made coffee. She seemed terrified of losing control, yet occasionally her mind and body betrayed her and she seemed to lose a sense of who and where she was. Perhaps that was why I grew up watchful and fearful for her, absorbed in her terror and yet excluded from her life. I watched, wide-eyed and speechless, as she retreated every night to bed in the large master bedroom, alone.

My father slept in my bedroom for a while. He didn't want me to be afraid of the dark, he said. It was during this period, when I was still in elementary school, that I became aware of vague sexual overtures on his part. They were not exactly overt, but he enjoyed it when I slept with him part of the night, and he and I took occasional overnight trips together. He liked to hold me in his arms.

On the face of it, there was no real impropriety. Yet I grew increasingly ambivalent and uncomfortable about his behavior. I sensed my father's loneliness but was embarrassed by it and by the intimacy he craved. By the time I entered junior high school, he retreated to the small baby bedroom where he remained until Susan and I left home permanently. He and I became courteous but guarded strangers.

My departure from home came sooner rather than later. At 13, I attended boarding school. Susan had become a distressed, unresponsive teenager, going dutifully to college after five years as an indifferent high school student. Perhaps we both felt discarded, although we never discussed this with one another—we had never communicated except

31

through anger and recriminations. My mother seemed relieved to see us go, my father disinterested.

Growing up became increasingly difficult. I attended university—dropping out twice—and went on to graduate school which, again, I never finished. These were shaky years for me. I had no idea what I wanted to do, where I wanted to go. Then came the unwanted pregnancy after a three-year affair with a rock musician who immediately married someone else. My parents were horrified and coped with the trauma by pretending it was not there. During the pregnancy, I worked as a domestic. The baby, a healthy eight-pound boy, was given up for adoption.

For a few years I worked as a clerk, then a teacher's aid, and, finally, a stagehand. My parents and I hardly communicated with one another. I heard that my sister had married, had a son, and moved back with my parents, but I had no idea how the arrangement was working out.

After years of professional meandering, I returned to graduate school, completing an MFA in theatre arts which enabled me to support myself acting, writing screenplays, and critiquing. It was a meagre living, but I was independent and doing what I wanted. Unexpectedly, I met Hank, a divorced filmmaker with a grown son and daughter. We decided to marry and combine our talents collaborating on documentaries. It took time, but it worked.

I saw my parents only occasionally during these years, and there was still an awkwardness between us. However, they liked Hank. And they were undoubtedly relieved to see me settled and looked after, finally, by someone else.

As I retrace the various stages of my life on the plane trip home, I am aware of how only in recent years have I begun to understand the difficulties of my parents' lives— my mother's depression, years of untreated melancholy, my father's isolation, and their bewilderment over what was happening to them.

Also, there must have been a terrible lack of resources then: Middle-class people did not seek out psychiatrists; they did not get divorced, except in the most extraordinary circumstances; it was considered bad taste to confide in one's friends and neighbors; and parents were expected to be dutiful, orderly, and, above all, respectable.

Within these constraints, my mother and father reacted badly as parents. It took me a long time to reconcile myself to this. Yet, with time and good counselling—about ten years' worth—I learned to expect less from them, both in looking back and looking ahead. I began to see my mother on her own terms, accepting, finally, that the bonding that should have been there when I was born was, quite simply, absent. What bound us over the years was a kind of mutual exasperation.

As for my father, I let go of a sense of disgrace over things past. Somehow, the unsettling aspects of our earlier intimacy receded as I began to see his attention as desperate but well-meaning. Even now I sense his past isolation, his need for human contact, the entrapment both he and my mother must have felt as they became more alienated from life and from one another. As their despondency became more apparent, so did the need for forgiveness. And as my life stabilized, the forgiveness came more easily.

Twenty years earlier, I wanted my mother and father to make things right for me. I resented it when they couldn't.

Now, instead, I have created my own world, one in which my parents will not fail me because I have substituted other, more stable figures. Although I can never shake off a sense of loss, a sense of absence of family, I make better choices with my life—a good husband, friends, roots.

Finally, I am returning to my mother and father, seeing them for what they are and for what they never will be. I see them as people, not just as parents.

And in so doing, curiously, I am no longer afraid to love them.

They are waiting for me, sitting and waiting in the living room, and they look as if they have been waiting a long time. Perhaps they have. It is nine o'clock at night. My father greets me at the door because he has heard the taxi draw up; he kisses me on the cheek and looks embarrassed but pleased. My mother does not seem displeased—she smiles wanly and says hello, offering her cheek—although she is frustrated that she cannot get out of her chair. There is a walker beside her.

They look old and fragile, but they are carefully dressed in immaculate clothing. I sit down, exhausted, and attempt to absorb their frailty. No matter how hard I try, I can never properly steel myself for it. Each time it gets worse. We make polite conversation for an hour. Neither my mother nor my father appears in any hurry to go to bed. I silently note that they are hungry for my company because they are, in fact, hungry for anyone's company.

Still, I don't mind. I need them to know that I'm there for them. If it has taken more than three decades, it doesn't matter. It seems unbelievable that the three of us can sit together and can listen to one another and still be of use to one another. Better late than never.

Finally, we get ready for bed. I carefully observe how long and painstaking their efforts are: my father helping my mother (using her walker) to the stairwell, my mother half crawling up the stairs and taking more than a full minute to reach her bedroom—still the same master bedroom—from the top of the stairs, a distance of seven feet. My father, stooped and with tentative movements, pulling down the bedclothes for my mother, putting a nightcap of port beside her bed. Finally, they close the doors to their respective bedrooms and I go back downstairs.

Alone in the living room, I look around and see that nothing is any different, the same dark, heavy furniture, Victorian leftovers from my grandparents, worn Persian carpets, the scratched hall table, zinc-like walls that remind me of jaundice.

I hear my mother above me, crossing the room with the aid of her walker: thump creak, thump creak, thump creak. It is an awful sound. I think of her life and of my father's and I am reminded of a line by TS Eliot: *I have heard the mermaids singing, each to each/ I do not think they will sing to me.*

I take a sleeping pill and go to bed.

I spend two weeks with my mother and father and, as much as it is possible, we become reacquainted. During this time I see only two other people. One is Lech, the Polish man and a widower who does light housekeeping for my parents several hours a day. Sixty-ish and sweet-natured, he drives with a plastic statue of Jesus on his dashboard and asks what my sign is. I like him. He is incredibly patient with my parents, listening carefully to everything they say.

I enjoy our many solitary talks in the kitchen. Each time Lech is quick to say how hard both my parents are trying, how difficult life is for them. Once I hug him in gratitude, even though his words depress me.

Maybe he is the only one who can give my parents the unconditional love they require, an employee who is paid minimum wage to tend to their needs six days a week.

The other person who comes is my parents' physician, Dr. Rosenthal, a man in his late 50s who makes housecalls. He appears the second morning of my visit. Not only has my father been having shortness of breath and dizziness, both he and my mother have decided to give him copies of their Living Will and Durable Power of Attorney for Health Care documents. My father has done his homework. Even my mother seems slightly more animated as she takes charge of her affairs. I do not want to be trapped, she says, waving one arthritic hand in the air.

They complete the papers—one forbidding extraordinary treatment (I don't want *any* treatment, my father says gruffly) unless authorized by them, and the other, the Durable Power, in which Susan is appointed the proxy decision-maker in case either parent becomes incompetent. Despite rumors that Susan is an alcoholic and rarely in touch with my mother and father, she lives nearby compared with the long distance between them and me. Besides, there is no one else who might be suitable.

Dr. Rosenthal is gracious and unhurried, spending time first with my father, warning him that if the dizziness continues, he will have to be hospitalized for tests and treatment. I don't need any of that, my father says, grimacing; I just want to be allowed to bow out. *My way.* Rosenthal is hesitant, conciliatory, a little embarrassed. I sense he doesn't disagree with my father, but, as a doctor, doesn't know what to say or do. This is the first time I have heard details of my father's deteriorating health. In all his letters, he has only referred to my mother's arthritis and paralysis.

Turning to my mother, Dr. Rosenthal is unusually solicitous, enduring her complaints with the patience of someone recently sainted. She wants to be happy, she wants to have fun, she wants to do all the things she used to do. She can't stand the walker, the physical therapist, the weather, she goes on and on as Rosenthal smiles benignly.

I want us to be like we were, she says, or not at all.

I am mesmerized by the conversation. It's the first time I have heard both my parents speak about how they feel, especially my mother.

Poor Rosenthal. He tries to console her by reminding her of all she's capable of doing, but she is not listening. She is not listening to anyone. I can see Rosenthal slowly retreating and mentally I retreat a few steps too, because my mother makes me nervous. She is alienating everyone who is capable of helping her. Soon there will be no one left.

To everyone's relief, I change the subject, showing my parents' directives to Rosenthal. I suddenly become businesslike and firm, a strategy I adopt when embarrassed, outlining the gist of both documents with the precision of a prosecuting attorney. Indeed, Rosenthal asks when I am finished, Are you a lawyer?

Still, he doesn't say it unkindly. He seems relieved that we have been so explicit about treatment, adding that such documents help everyone know where the patient stands. He seems to want to talk, mentioning cases of old, sick people kept alive against their will. We're savages, he says coolly, and goes on to describe aging relatives in a nursing home. Why am I still alive? one of them asks.

Nursing homes? my father says wearily.

Rosenthal names two, but adds that there is a long waiting list. You should have looked into this earlier, he says as he gets up to leave, suggesting that my parents contact a local social services agency to explore other alternatives. One is a live-in housekeeper, although, apparently, they're difficult to find.

As I see him to the door, I ask Rosenthal about the cost of either nursing home, and am overwhelmed at the rates he quotes. In one instance, a resident signs over two-thirds of his savings; the money becomes an advance down payment.

It strikes me that the arrangement is like a sinister bet: We're betting you, the resident, that you won't outlive what your payment would have covered. Isn't that encouraging the nursing home to nudge people out of the way before their money runs out? I ask.

Rosenthal shrugs and defends this particular residence, although he concedes that in less well-run places, abuses could occur.

It dawns on me that surviving when you're old is even more complicated than I had imagined.

For two weeks, our daily routine never varies except for Sundays, Lech's day off. Every morning my father gets up at seven o'clock and makes coffee and breakfast for my mother. I lie in bed and listen to the sounds of everyday life directly beneath me: the opening and shutting of the front door to get the newspaper, the kitchen faucet groaning (the plumbing hasn't been updated since the house was bought), empty coffee cups set on the dining room table, the same old oak table we have eaten off of for as long as I can remember.

Then silence.

Then thump creak, thump creak, thump creak from my mother's room and her slow descent downstairs. I have learned to sleep with my door open, and it's easy to hear the conversation in the dining room.

Well, how did you sleep? my father asks.

Oh. (Pause.) Not so badly.

Good. (Pause.) How do you feel?

Oh. (Pause. Sigh.) About the same. And you?

(Sigh.) I wake up too often.

There is another silence. Then my mother launches into a litany of complaints about her bowel habits. My father occasionally murmurs sympathetically. They are one another's only audience, locked into an intimacy that is, I think, embarrassing for them. Still, it is all they have and, as I will come to realize, it's a great deal.

I get up at eight or eight-thirty and go downstairs to have hot cereal and tea. My mother tells me I don't eat enough. My father becomes more upbeat when I am there, although conversation is choppy; I'm not at my best in the morning and say so.

My mother and I then go back upstairs to dress. The paralysis has affected her speech (now slurred); that and the arthritis hamper her body movements, but she can dress herself, even if it takes a long time. She makes up her face, unaware of the grotesque effect of brown pencil on faded brows and boysenberry lipstick tracing lips that are hardly there any more. Her clothing is, thanks to Lech, starched and fresh except for the same pair of shabby brown pumps that keep her from slipping. My father stays in his pajamas.

Every day is the same. I have a glass of sherry with my mother before lunch while Lech makes the beds and does the laundry. Then I take my mother for a drive in the car, a ten-year-old unadorned Buick with a mind of its own; it wanders all over the road and its fuel gauge and speedometer jump unpredictably back and forth.

After the ride I play Scrabble with her while my father naps. At four o'clock the three of us watch an hour of soap operas and at five o'clock I set the table and make dinner. At five-thirty, we sit in the living room, have a drink and talk for an hour until dinner. Afterward, my mother plays Scrabble by herself and my father reads. We are all in bed by nine-thirty and I read until I fall asleep, not always easy.

When my mother and I go on our drives, we talk of nothing in particular. She complains a good deal—she is bitter about the lack of attention from Susan and her son, as well as from neighbors. She says she wants more to do, have more company, more card games, go to more movies. Of course, what she means is more attention. Certainly the neighborhood seems more isolating than when I grew up; there are many fences, fewer children, more distancing. No one waves or acknowledges us as we come and go, although they can see us clearly.

I try to get more out of my mother—Does she follow the news? Is she reading any books? Does she want to do any travelling?—but she clings to the present, which means bemoaning the fact that my father cannot provide her with more stimulation. I keep reminding her that he is 80 and feeble, but she doesn't appear to hear me.

However, our conversation is more expansive before dinner, with my father something of a catalyst. I realize how much they want to talk, and I ask my parents to tell me about their upbringing, what it was like living through two wars and the Depression.

They also tell me about their lives during the last twenty years, a period when I was largely absent: my mother's job, something I was hardly aware of, my father's retirement, their daily routine, especially after my sister moved to her own house. Your father did all the housework while I was working, my mother says. My father smiles sheepishly. I walked two miles almost every day, he replies. They describe a trip to England, one to Western Canada, another to Scotland.

It is during these talks that I realize two things. The first is that my parents have had more of a life together than I had ever imagined. Before my visit, I had defined their marriage solely in terms of my exposure to them the first 20 years of my life, forgetting that lives, even difficult and mismatched ones, can evolve and bond in ways that are unlikely.

It was during this time, when I had left home and was hardly in touch with them, that my mother found an identity of sorts in a low-paying, lower-echelon job that marriage and motherhood had failed to give her. My father discovered he enjoyed being a househusband, and (I suspect) experienced a newfound attention and gratitude from his wife. No longer the breadwinner dependent on her for cooking, cleaning and ironing, he became the domestic partner and sounding board. Their lives centered around his two-mile walks, my mother's job, her complaints, and their yearly vacations. They had no friends.

In looking back, maybe they didn't want any. There was, during this period, a dovetailing of two lives, bound not by sexual intimacy, but by the intimacy that comes from long-term familiarity and resignation. Twenty years ago, my parents were old enough, or cynical enough, to know that nothing else would come of their lives. Whatever vision they might have had was buried beneath layers of lost illusions.

It is this that they have always shared—not a sense of what might have been, but an awareness that, very simply, that was the way things would be.

I think it was the perished hopes, hopes prompted by one another in the beginning, that, ironically, bound them so tightly the last 20 years. As they sit and recount the last few decades of their lives, there is no longer any separateness. Their identities are as intricately woven together as two figures on a netsuke.

Or, more to the point, two people caught in a psychological and cultural stalag. They have had no choice but to plod on, like blinded bisons.

Together.

Of course, the second thing I realize during our conversations is that all our talk is a prelude to what we dread speaking of, but why I am there: What will happen to my parents the rest of their lives? It is over a week before my father and I actually fall into the topic, when I casually mention nursing homes in the area. In a tone of voice that is childlike in its plaintiveness, he asks, Should we have gone into a **nursing home?** He pauses before adding, What **should we** do?

I cannot look at him. I think of my dream, in which he cries uncontrollably. For the moment, which seems interminable, it is impossible to respond because of all the emotions I feel. Then, finally, to mask an overwhelming sadness I become practical, but it is an agitated practicality. I ask my father what alternatives he and my mother have. I ask which ones are feasible, and, most important, I ask which one would be something they would be "happy" with. My mother looks away and announces that there is a television program that she wants to watch. She thumps briskly into the next room with her walker and turns on the television, leaving the door ajar.

My father sighs and says that the house, the stairs, and even the short distances between rooms have become overwhelming. I don't say so, but I know he is frightened.

Do you want to stay at home? I ask. He answers Yes without an instant's pause.

Are you sure? I say and he answers Yes again, adding, No hospitals, no nursing homes.

I finally say it, swallowing hard.

Did you mean what you said about the pills? I ask.

I wonder if my mother can hear us.

He nods.

45

Taking a deep breath, I tell him it's possible to get barbiturates from a European pharmacy, adding that they are stronger than Seconal and will ensure a peaceful and rapid dying. I am quick to say that I am not recommending anything, but that maybe the knowledge that he and my mother have recourse to this "source" might help them feel less helpless and less frightened. I quote the woman with MS: They're my insurance.

Maybe it will encourage you to hang on as long as possible, knowing you're really in charge, I say quickly, a little terrified that I have actually told him as much as I have. I gulp down half my drink.

Yes, it's better than the car exhaust, he says, and then asks for the phone numbers "when the time comes." He seems relieved and talks about the physical burdens, his and my mother's loss of control and their continuing isolation. Susan isn't around any more, he says; she and her son have lives of their own.

I wonder if he's too diplomatic to include me in the ones who aren't around. It's no secret I have always been careful to distance myself from them. Was it desperation that drove him to confide in me? Whatever the truth, I'm there. Maybe we are all desperate—he, my mother, and I—knowing that death is not far away.

Our conversation that evening veers in several different directions but ends on a positive note. I agree to give my father the phone numbers soon, when he asks for them. There is a certain reluctance on both our parts to actually exchange the information then and there. Instead we decide that he and my mother will stay at home and find additional help for the evening hours.

I write down a list of things that will make life easier—a reclining chair for my father, an electric moving chair for the staircase, a portable telephone, more games for my mother. I sense an interim period for my parents and perhaps my father does, too. I still cannot believe that I am there to negotiate the end of their lives.

I urge my father to talk more openly to my mother, subconsciously hoping that it will all go away. He shrugs and says he will try, but he doesn't seem hopeful.

As I get up to put dinner on the table, I peer into the room where my mother is watching television. She is watching a program called The Dating Game.

Somehow, I think, there is an apologue in this.

Three days before I'm scheduled to leave Philadelphia, Hank calls, sounding tired and frantic. His only brother, Warren, crossing a street in Dallas, has been hit by a van. There are head and chest injuries which affected oxygen to the brain. Can I come back earlier while he flies to Texas?

It takes me a while to respond and when I do, I'm not proud of my reaction. I resent this emergency in a way that's hard to conceal from Hank. Warren has been such a difficult, complex person, discarding wives and children as if they were trifles; in the midst of my concern for my parents, this latest crisis seems like an imposition. I'm too tired to pretend otherwise.

Also, it's hard for me to believe that Warren might die. Not only has he always seemed invincible, I have buttressed myself against the possibility of any other complications in our lives. For the moment I have to believe we are all immortal—Hank, me, my parents, Warren. What is happening is not really happening.

Still, I telephone the quadriplegic, my original excuse for travelling East, and cancel our interview, arranging to fly home the next day. My parents appear genuinely sorry that I'm leaving and in a way I am too. Somehow a closeness has emerged between us in the two weeks, not just with my father but with my mother, who is predictably distant but whom I understand better. I see her isolation as a way of shielding herself from a world that has become too chaotic, too bewildering. Perhaps it has always been that way for her, only now it is moreso.

On my last afternoon, I wash her hair in the kitchen sink, and I am struck by the smallness of her skull, like an upside-down bowling pin. She struggles to keep her balance as she leans over, and I resist the urge to put my arms around her and tell her that I love her, that I know life has not been easy for her. This would startle her, I know. Instead, I style her hair and make up her face and play Scrabble with her. She spells zygote on a triple word score and beats me by 213 points.

I leave the next day, promising to send my father the information he wants when he asks. My mother doesn't appear to know—or care about—what we're referring to. As the taxi waits outside, I get up to say goodbye and start to cry. My mother tries to stand to receive my embrace, by now a little emotional, but loses her balance and falls back into the wing chair. Her goodbye is vague and unfocused, but her goodbyes have always been vague and unfocused.

My father walks me to the door. He is dressed in navy trousers, white T-shirt, and a black-watch plaid shirt. I know the clothes are a tribute to me. As we stand at the front door, I give him, for the first time in my life, a full-frontal, unrestrained embrace. I can feel him crying against me.

I am crying too, but I manage to blurt out the one thing I have never said before: I love them, I say, and am proud of them. He clings to me as I turn to go. I cannot look back. What strikes me more than anything is that my father, my robust, sturdy father, has shrunk. Hugging him was like hugging a pygmy.

On the way to the airport, a familiar song sounds on the radio. For the first time I listen to the lyrics:

> They say there's a heaven for
> those who wait,

Some say it's better but I say
  it ain't . . .
And only the good die young.

Let me say a word here about my marriage.

On the whole, it's been a good one. Hank is a sweet-natured, loyal man who in many ways goes through life with blinkers on. He knows what he wants, goes after it, and ignores wayside hurdles. If people betray him, he has an admirable ability to forget them. He is incapable of carrying a grudge.

This probably comes from being orphaned early in life, forced to survive with Warren, two years older. Emotional resilience was a good defense mechanism in a string of foster homes, not all of them bad. Life was something one simply got on with. At 15 Hank fled to the city, where he worked for magazines and local television studios; he was determined to be a writer and filmmaker. That eventually he made it doesn't surprise me. I have always known that beneath the calm is a fierce, if understated, determination.

In his mid-twenties he married his first wife, had a son and daughter, and remained married until his wife divorced him to go to graduate school. Hank describes the marriage as happy, loyal, and gratifying while it lasted. That they remained good friends until she remarried didn't surprise me either. Nor did it bother me. Hank prefers a lack of disruption to anything else.

After a decade together, our marriage has gone pretty well. Hank and I moved slowly toward our goal of working together, something that attracted us when we first met years before. In a world of high risks and dubious payoffs, we seemed to balance out and cushion one another effectively. Unable to have children, we used our freedom to travel, experiment with our work and broaden our professional bases. There was some fun, some impulsiveness, and a good deal of hard work that, in time, paid off.

Between us, a pattern has emerged and remained: I research and write, Hank writes and produces. Notwithstanding some prickly moments, the teamwork has paid off.

In March, when I return home and Hank is still in Texas, we are in the final throes of finishing the "handicapped" film and scheduled to promote another documentary on capital punishment. Although both are works we're proud of, I find I never want to confront another disabled person or death-row inmate as long as I live. I have fantasies about fleeing wholeheartedly back to acting, throwing myself into comedy and farce. I am desperate to escape to another time, place, era, and identity.

Yet none of it works. I am neck-deep in reality. And nothing prepares me for the two months ahead or the last time I will return to Philadelphia.

Hank telephones the evening I return home to tell me that Warren has suffered massive brain damage; he is on life-supports and his wife and children want them removed. I cannot bring myself to ask if he will die. There is a long silence. Finally Hank says, There's not enough brain activity to sustain his breathing, so this way, taking him off the respirator, he'll go in peace.

I can't believe this is happening.

The supports are removed. Warren dies four hours later. Hank phones the following morning to say he will try and see Will, his son who is by now in prison, on the way back. He doesn't ask about my parents.

Coming home, he says, in neutral tones.

I look forward to his return, yet I dread it too. Suddenly I am tired of Hank's family. I am tired of all families, even my own. However, resent them as I might, over the next two months before my final trip to Philadelphia, all our relatives will unwittingly compete for our time and energy. The effect on Hank and me will be overwhelming.

In fact, the two-month period unfolds like an impossible obstacle course. For the moment, there are no longer any good times. The spectre of my parents hanging over me, I function much of the time in a daze. When Hank returns, he appears to have been punctured.

We go through life's daily routine by rote, coping admirably on the surface but feeling a crumbling of some vital underpinning in our lives. I dream that I am on a highwire and someone has removed the safety net. Hank is standing on the sidelines, watching impassively as the net is slowly dragged away.

A few weeks later, in the midst of final interviews with quadriplegic patients, my father telephones. Things are very bad here, he says. I wonder if you could help us. *Now.*

I take a deep breath as he tells me about the latest catastrophe. It seems that several nights earlier, at 10 PM, he got up to go downstairs. Why, I never discover. Turning the bend in the staircase, he lost his balance and fell, head-first, face-down, and upside-down, still on the stairs. He could not move, nor could my mother hear him; her bedroom door was closed. I had visions of lying there all night, he says to me in a small voice, and I didn't know what would happen to me.

Eventually my mother heard his calls and managed, with the walker, to open her door. Agitated, she telephoned the next-door neighbors, who have a key. However, the door was double-locked. My mother then called my sister, who lives a mile away, but she said she was without a car. Later, my father revealed that she was drunk.

Finally, my mother called the police. Breaking a window, they then unlocked the door and rushed my father to a nearby hospital for observation. He returned home the next day.

Never again, he tells me. Things have gone too far. His voice is about to break into the kind of sobs that only humiliation and fear can evoke. He pauses, collecting himself.

Then: Can you get me the pills now? he manages to say.

I feel as if my heart is breaking. I am sure my father's is. Yes, I say without thinking twice. There is a certain defiance in my voice, although who and what I'm defying is unclear. *Yes*, I say fiercely.

When I hang up, I am painfully aware of the shift in our relationship, a shift I have read about but never fathomed, when the parents are no longer parenting the child but the child parenting the mother and father. It's a sad and irreversible transition, discarding the final vestiges of daughterhood, childhood, being-taken-care-of security.

Suddenly (for it always feels sudden), there is nothing between you and full-fledged adulthood, no occasional lapses into childlike dependency.

No safety net indeed.

Six weeks pass. My father has agreed to wait until the pills arrive before making any further decisions. During this time, Hank's and my coping mechanisms falter even more, as if we are sinking in a quagmire. One bleak Monday morning, not long after my father's call, at my urging, we order the Vesparax from the European pharmacy. I know Hank is as tired of my family as I am of his, but he helps me place the order, feign a medical degree, sound appropriately doctoral. It works. Two weeks later they arrive, white aspirin-like pills in airtight aluminum containers. We are astonished.

The next morning I send 60 to my father in a plain brown envelope with no return address. I call him beforehand when I know my mother might be away from the telephone and ask him not to tell her about the pills' source or their existence. Better to say you've simply stockpiled them, I say. He agrees, although I urge him, as always, to talk to my mother about the way he feels. He says he'll try.

After I send the pills, I slip into a strange, uncharacteristic stupor. Not normally passive, I sit for hours at a time staring at the wall. I forget appointments; I don't answer the telephone. I agonize to Hank over losing my parents—the when, how, and where—I agonize like a broken record.

He, in turn, slips into his own despondency. At a promotional party we give, he cries over his brother's death and makes a pass at a girlfriend of mine. Everything's crumbling, I say to another friend, and she and I go off to a corner of our garden and weep under the trellis.

Hank leaves on his tour. I fill in for him occasionally and am absent-minded and distracted. Although I hate flying, I visit friends in faraway places, travelling and unburdening myself at a frantic pace. I resist returning home. When I do, there is a letter from Hank, who has come and gone in my absence. It is a letter I would like to forget.

We have argued over something, and in the letter Hank says he has reached a breaking point. We have drifted apart, he says, and he feels totally unsupported by me. He ends by saying that maybe we should separate. He can't concentrate, he can't work, he feels there is nothing to look forward to.

As I read it, I wonder if he isn't right.

He closes by saying that I have no monopoly on losing parents. Why can't you just get on with life and be done with it? he says.

It is a bad time for us.

I prepare for Hank's homecoming, feeling both terror and despondency. It is late April and the air is clammy and suffocating. I feel like even the weather is conspiring against us.

When Hank finally does come home, there is little fire, only despair. I realize, perhaps more than he, that we have been too submerged in our own distress to have been of much use to one another. Yet he suggests we keep on trying. We declare a truce, go out to dinner, listing the things that we still value about each other and the marriage (my idea). We make plans to go away for two weeks to a remote cabin in Colorado, our first holiday in over two years. It is a slightly uneasy cease-fire, but it is all we know how to do.

And, for the moment, all we have is one another.

Four days later, at five o'clock, my father telephones. On top of the dizziness, there is now bloating, which has become critical. He is threatened with drowning in his own fluid, which, in fact, almost happened. Rosenthal is sending me to the hospital for treatment tomorrow, he says, sighing bitterly. He has no idea how long he will be there, no idea how my mother will survive without him. If we pay Lech's relatives enough, (this with another sigh), maybe they can look after her in shifts.

There is a long pause. Should I do it now? he suddenly says. Should I take the pills tonight?

You can't leave Mother, I answer without thinking; not like that. You owe it to each other to talk this thing through, I add.

I feel desperate. I am also terrified.

He asks if it will be "too late" once he is hospitalized. I promise that we will get him out of the hospital if that's what he wants. We won't let you down, I say emphatically. He thanks me and sounds like a grateful child.

After he hangs up, I stare at the telephone for at least five minutes. I know the end is coming, I know that in some way I will be involved, and I am frightened. I also feel overwhelmed at the enormity of my responsibility, at the fact that I cannot turn back, nor can I turn away.

Finally I go outside to the garden where Hank is. I sit down and start to cry, sobbing with an abandon I haven't experienced since childhood. Perhaps this is the moment when we forgive one another. Hank looks at me and starts to cry too; he knows what is happening. I have to go to see them, I manage to say. I know, he says. We cry in one another's arms.

At that moment the barriers are gone. When we're able to speak, we agree that I should go to Philadelphia and look after my mother and touch base with my father. It's clear that neither Susan nor her son is involved in their care. She's not well, Hank says. You have to think of her that way or not at all.

We spend the evening booking a flight to Philadelphia; I get up at 5 the next morning to let my parents know I'll be flying over in 24 hours. They seem more relieved than I have ever heard them. I spend the day cancelling appointments, getting food in for Hank, doing the laundry. We cancel the cabin in Colorado.

At the airport, Hank and I share an emotional goodbye. Things between us are better. For the first time, he seems focused on what is happening between my parents and me. After all we've been through, I'm reassured by his final words of encouragement—that we must stand by my father, whatever he decides.

I need to hear that. For I know as I get on the plane that I am travelling all these miles to help my father die.

It's a long trip. Alone with my thoughts, my fears run wild with lurid scenarios. The principal one is an imagined attempt to free my father from unwanted life-supports, my dissolving (at his request) Vesparax into his orange juice and (again, at his request) removing the respirator feed lines. I fumble; the staff alerts the police. *Daughter toasts dad with death cocktail, snips life-line,* the headline reads. And in a subheading: *Sister claims suspect was always trouble-maker.*

I want to laugh and cry, and then I remember the old, terminally ill man I read about who was strapped to life supports against his will. He actually died that way. Tied down.

The plane lands. A taxi delivers me to my parents' house just after eight o'clock. An older, matronly woman has been with my mother, giving her dinner and waiting for me. As it turns out, she is Lech's sister-in-law and it was her daughter, anxious for the money, who spent the previous night with my mother. (Later I discover that she left my mother out in the rain as she sat indoors watching a soap opera.) It seems preposterous that this gregarious Polish family has become ad hoc caretakers instead of my sister and her grown son, but I keep my thoughts to myself.

The woman is relieved to see me and leaves right away. My mother seems relieved too, although she is even more vague and distant than usual. She tells me that my father was taken to the hospital the day before; she is worried about "what they will do to him."

Perhaps due to exhaustion, who knows, I sit facing my mother in the living room,

I face her and tell her with few preliminaries that my father is ready to go, that he wants to be allowed to die, that we must try to respect the way he feels. It's what he wants, I say.

She looks away from me as if she neither sees nor hears me. She won't focus on my presence.

My tone of voice is gentle enough, but the message is brutal. In looking back, I wish I had gone about it differently, more gradually, even though I wonder if my mother would have ever been prepared to hear me.

Finally, she murmurs noncommitally, still staring at lace curtains and zinc-colored walls and faded seascapes. I am suddenly reminded of a line from the play "Our Town" when I played Emily, who pleads with her mother to *Look at me, Mama, just look at me one minute.* I almost say the line out loud. Yet the moment dissolves in a sigh and a shrug.

We go to bed shortly after that, both of us tired and distracted. Nothing is resolved.

As it turns out, we will spend eight days together before my father comes home.

The pattern of our days is the same as it was during my last visit. I take my mother for rides, cook her dinner, wash her hair, and play Scrabble with her. Yet she receives my attention as something owed her, and against my better judgment I find myself craving thank-yous even though I know they will never come. Still, I talk less with her

60

about my father's wish to die, although I mention his long and full life. Typically, she murmurs and looks away. The aquarium-stare returns.

We talk to my father every day on the telephone. He is undergoing tests and "therapies" (whatever *that* means, he says angrily) and is uncomfortable and unhappy. His back is "thrown out" during a series of X-rays, an excess of laxatives has caused him to have several accidents in bed, and a ward mate—a Mr. dePalma—an elderly man who cannot speak, has had non-stop company every day, making rest impossible for the other patients. *This—is—hell,* my father says.

It's not until Wednesday, four days after my arrival, that I visit my father for the first time. Until then, he has been too exhausted for visitors. Now he feels rested enough to have company for an hour, he says. I'm nervous as I drive there in the wandering Buick, a hospital I had visited 20 years earlier. Now it's unrecognizable. The building looks like a huge etagere, not at all the friendly, three-story structure I once knew. After roaming through three lobbies, I take the elevator to the fifth floor, where all the patients are geriatric men. I walk past rooms where strange, primeval moans echo and where ashen relatives stand guard.

My father's ward is near the end of the corridor. I peek warily past the door and see him, finally, in the farthest corner. He is dozing. Approaching cautiously, I take a deep breath as I look down at him. He is still my father, but I cannot believe the final deterioration: He looks like a concentration camp inmate. He has shrivelled even more, lying vulnerable and unguarded, a scantily-fleshed skeleton, swollen belly, a full head of hair (a peculiar irony), shrunken limbs, hollow cheeks. There is an oxygen tube attached to his nose, and his mouth is slightly open. Oh Daddy, what have they done to you, I want to say, wanting to carry the frail skeleton, what's left of my father, away from the chrome and glass horror house.

But I can only stand and stare, choking back disbelief and an unendurable sadness.

I touch his hand and say his name.

He opens his eyes and sees me. He smiles.

My father remains in the hospital five more days; during that time I visit him every afternoon. We go to the nearby solarium where we look down at the Delaware River and talk privately. Not only am I relieved my father can walk; I'm grateful his mind is as clear as it is.

We sit and contemplate the river—occasionally a team of rowers strains against the current or a canoe glides downstream—while we talk about what he wants to do. There is absolutely no doubt about his goal, he says; he intends to die. It is less a desperate move than the logical conclusion to a life that has gone on longer than he has wished, he points out. Now there are the added complications of pain and further deterioration; delaying things will only make it worse.

We talk of particulars, and on Friday I tell him about a decision Hank and I have come to. If my father takes his life, we will assume responsibility for my mother. Without him, she is left stranded. Not only am I walking a delicate line in saying this, it's hard to believe I've come this far in acknowledging the possibility of my father's suicide.

However, with his continual talk about dying, all concerned with details of taking his own life, Hank and I have been shaken into certain realities. My father is absolutely determined now. In a sense, I've been swept into his determination like being swept out to sea in an undercurrent. Not only do I no longer have any say in his decision-making, there is no turning back.

After my departure, Hank made inquiries about nursing homes near us. There are, it seems, several possibilities. As I tell my father this, I stress that he shouldn't feel he is abandoning my mother. We'll make sure she's well looked after, I say. Looking down at the river, he says, I'm very, very grateful.

He then asks a question I already know the answer to but find almost impossible to verbalize. When would be the best time for me to take the pills? he says, this time looking straight at me.

I swallow hard. Now it's my turn to look away. Finally: You should do it while I'm here. I say in guarded tones. You can't leave Mother without anyone to look after her.

63

What is left unsaid is Susan's inability to assume any responsibility, nor do I mention the additional disruption of having to fly back again if my mother is left on her own. I feel like the compassionate executioner now, even though I have known all along that the timing of my father's plans is crucial.

Yes, he says, looking down at his hands. For once he doesn't ask if it would be an imposition.

Then: Rosenthal says I can be discharged on Monday, he says quietly.

In the middle of the week, Hank makes plans to fly to Philadelphia. It's no fun here, I say on the telephone, but he wants to come. Because of our cancelled vacation, he has nothing on his calendar and can arrange to fly in on Saturday.

I have mixed feelings about his coming and say so. Will the strain make our problems worse? I am so drained by my parents' dilemma that I can no longer think straight.

Yet my helplessness seems to spur him into action, and I sense his concern for the three of us. I also realize he might be trying to make amends. OK, I say. Not only do I want him there, it will be a relief to have someone other than my mother and Lech. Not surprisingly, there has been no contact of any kind from Susan.

By the time Hank arrives, death is just a week away. Each day brings something new, a new perception, an awareness, a development, another deterioration which, in looking back, become shards in our minds—mine, Hank's, my father's, even, I realize, my mother's—which, when pieced together, lead up to that night.

What happens, I realize now, become an inevitability.

Saturday night: Hank arrives at seven o'clock. I make dinner for him, my mother, and me. We are all quiet, conversation sporadic. My mother, usually more animated in his presence, is surprisingly uninspired. I have always known that she wonders what Hank sees in me: This won't last, was her sole comment when she heard we were married.

Yet she expresses no interest in him and retreats into a studied calm, reluctant to cheer up even when we promise to take her out to lunch the following day. Maybe she feels invaded by our presence and wishes instead that we were Susan and her son, who seem to have vanished from her life.

Hank and I are relieved to see one another, but cautious. Later, after we have all gone to bed, we lie in the dark, holding hands but not speaking.

Before I fall asleep, I review the scenario that is unfolding. It is too surreal, too bizarre, too unlikely. I feel swathed in gauze, as if I am viewing life and events through a scrim cloth. I cannot, do not want to absorb the horror of what is happening. When I do sleep, I dream that I am embalmed while still alive.

Sunday: Hank and I visit my father in the hospital before taking my mother out to lunch. My father is happy to see Hank; they have always had a cordial relationship. Yet it is difficult to talk. The ward is full of visiting dePalmas. There is too much noise, too few chairs. We speak of nothing in particular except my father's relief at leaving the next day.

When we drive away, Hank mentions his horror over the other patients, all of whom, because of strokes or heart attacks or chronic illness, are incapable of speaking. They just lie there, surrounded by hovering relatives, their only movement blinking eyes and fluttering hands, their only communication a gutteral sound.

We take my mother out to lunch at a 200-year-old restored inn. It takes her ten minutes to get from the back door of the house to the car. At the restaurant she nearly falls twice as she moves at a crawling pace with her walker through the lobby. It is a tedious, painfully slow lunch; both she and Hank are silent. When I remind her that she hasn't yet asked Hank how he is, she answers noncommittally that she had asked him that on his last visit. Silently, I note that his last visit was two years ago.

That evening Hank reveals that he is stunned to see how badly disabled my mother is. You don't see it so much in the house because she moves in such a small space, he says, but outside. . . . his voice trails off.

Monday: Hank and I leave at ten in the morning to pick up my father at the hospital. An orderly wheels him down to the parking lot. Despite his immaculate appearance— plaid shirt, black trousers, white cotton socks, espadrille slippers—he looks withered. Yet as we drive home, I get a chuckle out of him when I say that as a special homecoming present, we have imported the dePalma relatives!

My mother is waiting for us in her usual place at the dining room table. When my father walks falteringly in the door, what happens next will help me understand, more than anything, what is to happen the following Sunday.

It is simple: My parents embrace. I have never, in my entire life, seen them be demonstrative with one another. Not once.

Now they embrace, not a perfunctory, methodical embrace, but a spontaneous, and, for them, heartfelt hug. They kiss briefly and draw back and then embrace again. I avert my eyes (finally) and am dazed at this gesture of unexpected intimacy. Hank moves away, too. We are intruders.

During the afternoon some visiting nurses come, which my father resents. By now he hates anyone even remotely involved in the health-care profession. Also, a deliveryman brings an oxygen tank which should be available to my father at all times, a difficult feat considering the size of the house. More problems.

Lech comes and goes, and things seem unbearably chaotic. Hank and I pick up a wheelchair we have rented for my mother; she can no longer go any distance with her walker. My father, exhausted and on mild pain-killers, sleeps on the reclining chair downstairs, moaning occasionally in discomfort. He asks me to put a garbage bag underneath him in case he has an accident.

My mother grows increasingly frantic, complaining that my father will never talk to her, do anything with her, share anything with her. She becomes increasingly shrill, but I know that her irrationality is because she is terrified. In many ways I am, too.

Tuesday: In the morning, while I take my mother for a drive, Hank talks to my father. There is a rapport there, I think, because both men have an inherent sweetness. They also respect one another a great deal. And, because of the era in which he grew up, my father is probably more consoled by a man's presence than a woman's.

As Hank tells me later, my father says there is no doubt that he will take his own life. Three things have convinced him more than anything: his back pain is excruciating and stronger pain-killers would only aggravate his other health problems; he will not have strangers in the house caring for him or my mother; and, perhaps, most important, the impact of the other men in the ward— lifeless, desolate, totally helpless—has devastated him. Not for me, he says to Hank.

And then (beat): When would be the best time to do it?

With typical candor equalled only by my father's, Hank replies probably on a weekend, when no one else—no visiting nurses, Lech, doctors, or deliverymen—is around. (Later he will tell me that my father's practicality demanded such a response; he answered without thinking and was a little overwhelmed when it all came out.)

My father thinks for a minute and then nods. Yes, he says, that's true.

That afternoon Hank and I go to Dr. Rosenthal's; he has agreed to see us at four o'clock. We ask him pointedly what the prognosis is for my parents. Looking grim, he says that their conditions have deteriorated to the point where both my mother and father will either have to have round-the-clock home nursing care or be admitted on an emergency basis to a nursing home. No choice here, he says. Then he adds that if they refuse to have anyone in their home, they can have an alert button which notifies the town's paramedics in case of emergency, but this means they will automatically be hospitalized, whatever the problem.

If they refuse any of this, he says, they can die—especially my father—in ways that are prolonged and somewhat gruesome. He looks embarrassed, as if he is personally responsible for failing to give us a better answer.

It is then I say that my father has stock-piled drugs and is thinking of taking his own life. If he goes through with it, we will take my mother with us and care for her, I add. Hank notes that we have found several nursing homes not far from us that would take her in at a month's notice.

I cannot resist saying, aware that Rosenthal knows her, that my sister could have done more. She has problems of her own, he replies, and, once again, I have a sense of a disordered life, of pointless grudges and muzzled anger—toward my parents, toward her ex-husband, toward me, toward life.

Rosenthal suddenly asks if we have read Orwell's *1984*. Do you remember the part where people, when they reach a certain age, can go to die? It's peaceful, it's civilized, it's something I never forgot, he says.

Then he says: That's the way it should be.

Wednesday: Hank leaves at midday for Florida to complete a final interview, the only one left to do. He'll be back in two days.

After Lech has left, my parents and I sit in the living room. They ask what Rosenthal said to Hank and me the day before and I sum it up in two, maybe three alternatives: 24-hour home nursing care, or a medical alert button which ensures that paramedics will take them to the hospital if anything goes wrong. Neither my mother nor my father looks at me when I speak.

Maybe there's a third one, I say. Emergency admission to a nursing home, but I didn't think you were interested in that.

No, my father says. No more hospitals, no more strangers in the house. Then: What about just leaving us alone?

I shake my head and mention something I have thought out carefully. You can't do that to yourselves, I say. You can't do it to one another. You would collapse or choke or have a seizure, and where would that leave Mother? Or she would collapse and you would be utterly helpless.

It's a scenario I have imagined many times. I cannot let that happen to them.

My father shakes his head. *Boy,* my mother says, and I know she is angry.

I find myself apologizing as if, like Rosenthal, I share responsibility for what has gone wrong. I'm sorry, I say several times. I'm so sorry.

Neither of them appears to hear me.

Thursday: My father's pain has intensified. That morning he moans almost nonstop in his bedroom. I go in to close a window and I hear him mumble Go away. This frightens me. More than anything I am terrified he will lose control both mentally and physically. What then will happen? I realize now how much we have taken his plodding rationality for granted.

71

Later in the morning, after Lech has brought him downstairs, my father mentions that he thinks a conservatorship for my mother is a necessity if he dies first. She is unrealistic, almost paranoid about money, he says; he'll call the trustee of their estates later in the afternoon. I watch my mother watching us from the dining room and know that she will soon start yelling at my father for not talking to her instead of to me. She does. It dawns on me for the first time how jealous she is of me. She watches my father and me with a hawk's eye.

Dr. Rosenthal appears for an unexpected visit at four-thirty. We sit in the living room. His examination of my father is friendly but perfunctory. My father is polite but appears to have lost all interest in medical examinations.

Rosenthal then turns to my mother, who sits in the wing chair by the fireplace. He leans over her, bracing himself by putting both arms on the chair's wings. It is an intimate, affectionate gesture, as if he is embracing the chair because he cannot embrace her.

Expecting the usual litany of complaints, I start for the kitchen to put out the garbage and make dinner. However, I turn around abruptly when I hear her answer to his simple question. He calls her by name. Then: How are you?

We want to go together, she says. We're a burden. We have no future.

I forget the garbage and frying onions and watch her, transfixed.

There's no life for us any more, she says. It's time we went. We don't want to go on like this.

I can smell my onions burning. Rosenthal tries to sooth her by saying (helplessly, I think) that somehow something can be worked out.

No, she says, and shakes her head. No. No. No.

Friday: Early that morning I speak to my father about something that's been bothering me a great deal. Luckily he is out of bed, sitting on a chair. My mother is in the kitchen, well out of earshot.

You've got to talk to Mother some time, I say, adding, I feel as if your plans are being made around her. Silently I worry about the shock effect of my father's death if he has not prepared her.

He nods and agrees that late that afternoon would be a good time. There has been little time for them to talk, no time for them to be alone together. Either my father has been flat on his back because of the pain, or there has been someone else around—Lech, visiting nurses, deliverymen, my mother's physical therapist.

By lunchtime, when Hank returns, my teeth are on edge. I have spent the morning taking my mother for a drive in the country, promising to find a street where a former friend used to live. The traffic is too dense, I cannot properly read the map, I cannot follow street signs. The Buick wanders everywhere but where I want it to go. I never find the street, and my mother reacts as if I had lost the path to the Holy Grail.

From the moment we arrive home until lunch is over, she complains nonstop about my driving to the point where I go into the kitchen and cannot stop crying. I whisper to Hank that I can't take any more, that I had no idea how much she despised me.

We've got to see it through for your father's sake, he says.

Of course, he is right.

Hank and I leave the house from three forty-five until seven in the evening. I have left stuffed baked potatoes (something I have made every night for my parents; they like the recipe) and a meatloaf, which should be ready by the time we return. He and I go to a tavern next to the state mental hospital. We are surrounded by people using words like catatonic and fugue. Somehow, given the bizarre nature of what we are going through, the context of insanity doesn't seem inappropriate. Hank and I spend two and a half hours discussing how to handle my mother when and if my father takes his life, as well as which would be the best nursing home for her. By this time we have a list.

We arrive home just before seven o'clock. My parents are waiting for us at the dining room table. I serve dinner. For a while we make small talk, dancing around a subject that has to be kept at bay, at least for a little while. Between bites, I feel as if I am holding my breath. Finally, as we are finishing dinner, Hank asks rather neutrally if they have had a chance to talk. My father puts down his napkin and looks at us both, first one, then the other.

We have decided, he says, pronouncing each word slowly and deliberately, that we want to go together. I have made up my mind, I have told your mother, and it is her decision to go along with me. He sounds as if he is addressing a board room meeting.

I stare at my father, my mother, then at Hank, and back to my mother. I had not expected this. All along, I had been convinced of my mother's determination to keep going, to finally "have some fun" (something she has been saying for as long as I have been alive), as unlikely as that is.

She nods as if she has read my thoughts. Her lips are pursed. She looks grim but determined. Yes, she says. It's decided. We're going together.

I react in a way I had not anticipated. I start to cry, long, deep, convulsive sobs. I say things which surprise me, because a part of me, a more rational part, has always qualified such feelings: I tell my parents how much I love them, how much I will miss them, how I cannot imagine life without them. I am crying into my napkin, by now drenched and soggy. My father looks bewildered but moved, saying, somewhat awkwardly, Well, we've certainly made some mistakes. . . . and his voice trails off, embarrassed.

You're entitled to mistakes, I say, surprised at how quick I am to defend them, saying again that I love them and will miss them. This is only the third time I have told them I loved them (the first being at the end of my previous visit), and it makes me cry even more. Finally I go over to my mother and hug her, telling her that I wish life had been better for her. She nods stoically, enduring my embrace.

In the midst of my tears, Hank and my parents discuss the when and how. I'm not sure he believes them, but Hank has always coped with confusion by listening and not reacting. Sunday night—two nights away—is chosen. My parents feel they should clear up some matters and also tell Susan of their plans. My father gets up to call her, asking her to come by the following day between noon and two in the afternoon. He doesn't say why. Hank and I agree to take my mother out to lunch at this time.

My parents go to bed almost immediately. If anything, they seem tired but relieved, especially my father. For some reason, all my pity goes to my mother. I know my father is going to his death feeling as if virtually everything is resolved. He is ready.

But, for my mother, there is unfinished business, a lifetime of dissatisfaction, which makes her departure one with regrets. No one has ever made life right for her.

I put her to bed, spending extra time on her nightcap, her bedclothes, her air conditioner. Before taking her walker and helping her get in bed, I hug her lightly and kiss her on the cheek. Again, I start to cry. You're a brave person, I manage to say.

She is largely unresponsive, disengaging herself and getting into bed. Before I leave—I'm just about to shut the bedroom door—I hear her say to me, slowly and in carefully measured tones: I just want to say that your displays of emotion are (here she pauses; I catch my breath) . . . appreciated.

I turn and look at her, but she is staring at the wall.

I close the door.

Later, I will realize that this is my reward.

Saturday: It is a hectic day. It takes most of the morning to find a restaurant that has a good view, good parking and wheelchair facilities, and will please my mother. It isn't easy, but I finally find one. I am enormously relieved. After all, it is her last meal in a restaurant.

My parting words to my father are *not* to tell Susan where the drugs came from. My mother still doesn't know, and Hank and I prefer to keep it that way. We are both leery of my sister; for reasons I can never decipher, she has been angry at nearly everyone around her (including me) for as long as I can remember. None of this helps.

My father, by now overly protective of Hank and me, says crisply, That will be absolutely no problem. He is so emphatic I smile. I kiss him goodbye on the cheek. He says, as much to himself as to me, Your mother and I have seriously revised our opinions of your sister in the last few years. . . . I leave it at that and go out the front door. Maybe that was meant to be another reward.

It's a fine lunch. We are all on our best behavior, and my mother seems almost cheerful. Afterward we drive along the river to the graveyard where my mother's parents are buried. She has not been there in more than 20 years, but she knows exactly where to go. It is a beautiful, clear afternoon. I do not say so, but I wonder if my mother wants to say goodbye to her parents, on this earth, at any rate. Hank and I wheel her around in the wheelchair. We are, all of us, almost gay.

We arrive home around two-thirty. Susan's car is gone, and my mother's face suddenly looks like aspic that has fallen. Why couldn't she have waited to talk to me? she says over and over again. I'm not going to be around much longer.

How did it go? I ask my father.

Well, he says and pauses. I didn't mention *when* we were thinking of doing it, only that we were. Both of us.

And?

Again, a pause. She said she would respect my decision, but not your mother's. Pause. Then: She asked if you and Hank had put us up to this.

I feel totally defeated by Susan's words but manage to keep my mouth shut. I tell Hank later, who shrugs and points to his head. I don't laugh.

At dinner (again, stuffed baked potatoes with a tuna casserole) my parents, by now absolutely determined, say they want to be clear about details for the following evening. My father points out the importance of combining their overdose with a small meal taken with soda water and alcohol, as well as a seasick pill. I assume he has told my mother about his "stockpiled" barbiturates. Hank and I listen, speechless. We want to do this absolutely right, my father says. Absolutely right, my mother echoes like a creature from a Lewis Carroll novel.

But her response is, in fact, less of an echo and more of a declaration. She is asserting herself as I have rarely seen her do. Won't she reconsider and come with us instead? I ask. Won't they both? Now I don't want them to die; this is a bad dream. They shake their heads in unison. *No.* My father suggests that Hank and I go somewhere else for the Sunday evening so we won't be implicated. Hank agrees. We can check into a motel and can come back early the next morning, he says.

However, I balk and start to cry again. I cannot leave them to die alone. Although I don't say so, I am afraid that something will go wrong, that one of them will panic while the other lies dying, that they will die thinking that no one is there for them.

No, I'll stay, I say. Hank says nothing. I wonder if he can believe this is happening.

My mother keeps looking at the clock. Finally she says, She always calls at seven o'clock. It is now six-forty. She is speaking of

Susan. We all start staring at the clock. Six forty-five, six-fifty, then seven o'clock, and still silence. My mother looks distressed but says nothing. Seven-fifteen. Still nothing.

Finally at seven-thirty, my father telephones, asking if Susan can come over sometime the following morning. Yes, she can come before she goes to church, she says.

We all breathe a sigh of relief. My mother says nothing, her face aspic once again. I wonder if she feels humiliated because her final meeting with her favorite daughter has had to be arranged like a reluctant blind date.

After dinner, when my parents are in bed, Hank and I sit on the porch, drinking. It's no good, he says. With your sister feeling the way she does. . . . and he doesn't finish his sentence.

What do you mean?

He says that he will leave, that we should both leave because Susan is convinced that somehow, for whatever reasons, my parents are not acting independently. She can't be trusted, he says.

Then go, I say. I'm angry. I can't leave. I cannot leave my parents now. Things have gone too far. Go, I say again. And let's get a divorce.

I have two more drinks, get quietly, morosely drunk, and fall into bed at ten-thirty.

Sunday: At six-thirty in the morning, we are, the four of us, sitting around the dining room table. Perhaps I am too dazed to feel angry at Hank. Instead, I listen as he argues that he and I should be there when Susan shows up at nine o'clock. If she thinks we've put you up to it, he says to my parents, it's important that we have this final family gathering together. My parents murmur their disagreement. They're probably afraid of fireworks. Yet Hank persists.

I see his point and chime in my agreement. She has to see that it's *your* decision, I say, that we've urged other alternatives.

Finally it's agreed. We sit in silence, staring at empty coffee cups. My nervousness is overwhelming. At eight-fifteen I run upstairs and take two Valium. At eight forty-five her car draws up—an unimaginative, older-model, four-door sedan—and I hear her walking up the front path (I have my back to the front door and cannot bring myself to turn around), then the steps, now the screen door, and finally the front door. I look down at my hands and see perspiration literally dripping from them. I cannot look at Susan, partly in fear and partly in embarrassment; she had no idea Hank and I would be there. Stopping to shut the front door, she turns to face us and freezes. She then speaks our names in choked, shrill tones, an unsuccessful attempt to presume cordiality while blocking what must have been the most frenzied rage, like that of an animal caught in a trap. I say nothing.

She sits down at the table (what else can she do?) and I am suddenly aware of the curious seating arrangement, wholly un-planned. I am at the head of the table. My sister sits across from me in my mother's chair. My parents are in the "side" chairs, where Susan and I sat as children. Hank stands behind my mother.

Finally, I look at Susan. She is lighting a cigarette. In less than five seconds, my fear of her evaporates. Vanishes. Her hands shake, her voice trembles, her face, once consider-ably beautiful, is beefy and fallen. She cannot sustain eye contact. *She is lost,* is the phrase that repeats itself over and over in my mind.

I had anticipated many emotions, but never one of pity. In less than a full minute, I have experienced what feels like an epiphany. Susan has been victimized more than I had ever imagined. During the long years when I was away from home and family, it was she who remained trapped with my parents, ini-tially of her own volition and then, later, un-able to escape. There was nowhere else for her to go.

I say little. I don't wish to. Hank lets my parents present their own case, which they do eloquently. When I do speak, I fault Susan for not entering my parents' names on a wait-ing list of local nursing homes, but I don't dwell on it. I don't really want to look at her; she radiates the same throttled urgency my mother radiated for years, and in a moment of awful awareness, I realize the two are clones.

After an hour, Hank and I feel it's time to leave. There should be no doubt in Susan's mind now about my parents' intentions. He and I go for a walk, agreeing to return at noon. We know that my parents have chosen not to tell Susan they will carry out their plans that evening, just as they have specifically said they have no wish to see their grandson. There is a bitterness there that neither Hank nor I can resolve, so we let it go.

We get up to leave. I look in the hall mirror to comb my hair, glancing simultaneously at Susan. We are both dressed in green, she in an unadorned olive green shirtwaist dress (I guess LL Bean). My green is a sea-green Mexican blouse with fringe draped over plain white trousers. Despite the fatigue, my eyes are holding out well, and I murmur silent thanks to the Reebok team of miraculous cosmetic wizardry. Once Susan and I looked alike. Now no one would suspect we are even related.

In many ways, we are not. As Hank and I leave the house, I am aware of something that has defied all the odds, was not written into the script.

As unlikely as it may seem, I am the survivor in all this.

Hank and I stay away for three hours. We buy a *New York Times* and read it at a nearby park. Between sections, we speculate about what's happening at home. As Hank points out, Susan is now "implicated" by the fact that my parents have been so explicit with her about their plans. Maybe he's right, but she will always be an unknown quantity to me. To be on the safe side, we decide to check into a motel that afternoon while taking my mother for a final ride. We won't stay there, but just in case there is some question about our whereabouts after my parents have died, the motel isn't a bad idea.

At noon, when we return home, Susan has left. My parents are still seated at the dining room table. How did it go? I ask. OK, not badly, they say almost in unison. We didn't tell her when, my father adds, but she realized what we both intend to do. I guess she accepted it. My mother nods.

Did she kiss you goodbye? I ask, unable to curb my curiosity.

My mother does not answer. My father says, In a fashion.

My parents will live eight more hours. From the moment Hank and I return home, the four of us become totally submerged in the details of how to bring the afternoon and evening to a close. The practical side of my father takes over, and my mother, quieter, more watchful, follows his lead.

I think for all of us, those eight hours—and there was no turning back now—were like a dream. We walked, talked, planned, and took care of dozens of last-minute chores. However, none of it seemed real. There we were, immersed in the most mundane tasks, all of which were a preparation for the suicides of my mother and father. I had to resist the feeling that I was a player performing in an astonishing melodrama and occasionally losing my way, groping for footlights, casting directions, and cues.

Hank became dutiful. Having gone this far, he probably had no other choice. I simply kept moving. My mother lost her aquarium stare and surveyed everything with vigilant eyes, while my father pressed on with an energy that was prodigious, considering his age and health.

For him, life had become a bad dream, a nightmare which, now that it was decided was over, he couldn't leave soon enough.

2—3 PM: As planned, Hank and I take my mother for a ride in the country and, while there, register in a motel for the night, paying with Hank's credit card. We go into the room and quickly unmake the bed and dampen some towels to make the place look lived in. I tell Hank that he can stay there if he wants, but he says No, he'll see it through with me.

My mother, who waits outside in the car, says nothing about why we have been inside 20 minutes, even though she must have known. On the way home she comments on the brightness of the flowers and leaves and sky. It is a fine afternoon. There is no emotion in her voice as she speaks.

3—4 PM: Again, as planned, Hank takes my mother for a long walk around the neighborhood in her wheelchair. As discussed with my father, I take three-quarters of the

Vesparax and pulverize them in the Cuisinart. It is a long, wearisome job. The mixer exhales so much powder I wonder if I will be the first victim. Finally I put the powder (the equivalent of 60 Vesparax) into a cereal bowl in the china cabinet. Beside it are another 20 pills to be taken orally.

I then go in to join my father. He has been organizing bills to be paid, services to be cancelled, and resolving a mountain of other minutiae. I tell him about the clouds of dust from the Vesparax and we share a wry laugh. He likes the irony of that, and it occurs to me that I have never seen him so content or so well-organized—like someone who has planned for years to take a long and wonderful, much fantacized about trip and the time has finally come: passport, travelling shoes, wash-and-wear suit all in order.

What about a note? he says, and together we work out something appropriate. Finally, I sit across from him and type out my version of draft one. It's fine, he says; he'll copy it in his own hand, adding one or two things.

Hank returns with my mother, and she says she wants to sit in the wing chair by the fireplace. I put some "elevator" music on the radio—the only kind she can abide—and leave her while I show Hank the Vesparax in the kitchen. I ask how the walk went and he says it was tiring.

Your mother didn't seem to want to talk, he says. We stopped and spent 20 minutes sitting on the lawn of the elementary school.

I asked if she had any final thoughts, and her only comment was that the PTA had never appreciated her. Then she shut up.

4–5 PM: While my mother sits in the wing chair, I study her. In the background Mantovani is flamboyantly conducting "The Desert Song." My mother is oblivious to me. She is somewhere else, grim, resigned, sad, and frustrated. I know she is not ready to die, but she will never be ready to die because her entire life has been an accumulation of unhappy relationships, unfounded suspicions, endless regrets.

She has loved the wrong people. Her husband is leading her to the grave. The only son she had died in infancy. The daughter she loves has drifted away. Her only cousin, aged and partially senile, responds to an early morning phone call and comments about dying ("It's tonight. They say the pills will make it quick and painless") by asking about the weather. The daughter who remains with her at the end is not the one she would have chosen. They have never gotten along. She wishes she would go away.

I know my mother is thinking this. She stands up abruptly at one point, making a choking, sobbing noise, and then falls back in her chair. I go over and hold her hand, and all she can say is, I can't—I can't absorb this.

Almost in a trance, I go up to the attic without thinking and bring down three boxes full of photographs of her family. I pull up a chair beside her, and for 45 minutes we go through every picture of her parents, of her and her sister as children, their pets, their friends. I am more interested in the albums than she is, but, like an all-suffering tour guide, she fills me in on details when I ask. Nothing about the pictures (and there are some wonderful ones) appears to move her.

When we finish, she says dryly, My parents were wonderful people.

5–6 PM: At five o'clock, Hank and my father join my mother and me in the living room. The two men have spent the previous hour finishing business matters: Hank writes out checks for bills that are due and my father signs them. My father gives him details of how their estate should be settled, and he renews his membership in AARP. Also, in a wonderful last touch, he bills Hank and me for all long-distance phone calls made since we have been there, but reimburses us for our plane fares. Finally, all is in order.

We sit facing one another in the living room now and I am dying for a drink. *Shouldn't we all have a drink together?* I say eagerly, glancing at my parents, who look as if they are in the middle of some strange ritual and haven't the vaguest notion what to do. They nod. Hank goes into the kitchen and brings back a bottle of Champagne from a relative's wedding; he pours four glasses and hands them around. My mother looks at the extended glass and says, I—don't—like—Champagne.

I honest-to-goodness work hard to suppress a guffaw and go to the kitchen, mixing her a gin and tonic. I am torn between laughing and crying; we are in the midst of the most somber and possibly gruesome scenario (not excluding the possibility that Susan will drop in unexpectedly), with none of us saying or doing what we should be doing. This should be a time of embracing, gentle tears, and final thoughts. Instead, we are behaving like four adolescents on a double date, ossified into a stupified silence.

Finally my father breaks the ice by saying—clearing his throat, looking away from us to screw up his courage—Your mother and I want you to know that we are extremely grateful to both of you for all you have done for us. I don't know what we would have done without you. It is a speech. I realize he has probably memorized this.

He still looks away. He cannot say more. But I recall the expression on his face in a picture when he held Susan as an infant: as if something strange and wonderful had happened to him and he didn't know how to respond.

Because my mother and father seem to have no desire to say anything, Hank and I ask them if there is anything in particular they would like us to do—special burial procedures, last-minute bequeathments, a funeral or memorial service? They are adamant about the latter and say No in unison, lapsing into temporary grumbling as they abhor the hypocrisy of those pretending to mourn them in death when they had been so negligent in life. By "they," I assume they mean Susan and her son as well as their neighbors. There isn't anyone else left except me, and I wonder if I have been included in the editorial "they" but will never know.

Before we go in for supper my father smiles a little sheepishly and asks my mother if she remembers "that time" on Chesapeake Bay? She looks blank, but he reminds her, as he puts it: In a moment of passion, we stood out on that jetty, and—don't you remember?—I put my arm around you and said that it was so beautiful that that was where our ashes should be scattered.

My mother seems to remember (I think so, she says vaguely), signalling in her understated way that that would be all right with her, but I wonder if she really cares. Can she remember, or does she even want to remember, my father's outburst in such an uncharacteristic moment of abandonment?

It would appear not, but I am comforted by my father's recollection of it, the remembrance of his excited declaration and hearty embrace of his then-young wife. It is curious how, the closer my father comes to death, now two hours away, the more in touch with life he becomes.

6 PM: We go in for supper, which I have meticulously planned (for once, no baked stuffed potatoes; this time, leftover tuna cas-

serole). The table's seating arrangement has once again changed, with Hank now at the head of the table, my mother at the other end, and my father and me in the side chairs. More than anything, now that the preliminaries are over (which possibly embarrassed them), my parents seem keen to "get on with it."

But I cannot let them go quite yet, and I tell them (now through tears) that they have much to be proud of, and I hope that they will take that with them. They look at me a little blankly. Through sobs, I reiterate that they have had two healthy children, a healthy grandson, a nice house, nice jobs, I have married a nice man, we have worthwhile careers, I say all this, I realize, not only to elicit some final blessing from them, but also to make them feel they are ending their lives with a sense of accomplishment. Not surprisingly, my father smiles his bemused smile— Yes, we appreciate what you say, he says diplomatically. Maybe he believes me. My mother murmurs noncommittally.

Pause.

Well, my father says, pushing himself away from the table. I think we should get on with it.

I cannot reconcile myself to this final shift, this about-face, and I dart into the kitchen where I swallow in one gulp a three-ounce shot of bourbon. That my parents should go so calmly to their deaths is something so painful and unnatural I feel as if the wind has been knocked out of me. They have utterly surrendered now, and I am painfully, woefully unprepared.

It's clear now: My mother and father are going to orphan me. For all the terrible rifts that have existed between us, for all the unfinished business that I had hoped would be put to rest and wasn't, they are still my mommy and daddy and I am somewhere back in ankle socks and braids and a blue taffeta dress with a maroon sash, and they are there to look after me and live forever.

So I take another gulp of my father's Kentucky bourbon, dry my eyes and steady my hands, and go back out to the dining room to ask: How would you like your Vesparax?

7 PM: It is decided. My father will dissolve his portion of the pulverized Vesparax in 7-Up and warm applesauce; my mother in 7-Up and coffee ice cream. They will each take ten pills orally beforehand, and then "eat" and "drink" the rest. The dosage they will ingest is three times what is normally considered lethal.

Knowing that Hank and I will be there to help them, knowing that they are so close to death, appearance and pretense fade as my mother and father become slightly childlike and a little concerned about decorum. Should we stay down here? Should we go upstairs? Should we change our clothes?

Resisting the urge to say that this is one ceremony for which Emily Post has no prescribed etiquette, I suggest that the best thing is for them to be as comfortable as possible, so why not put on bedclothes and simply go to bed? Yet I cannot resist asking if, just this once, they would not prefer being together (I do not say it, but I know that they know I mean in the same bed). They demur. With Victorian primness they say No, they'd both prefer being in their own beds. I find this decision painful but predictable. Later, I will berate myself for having believed that such entrenched patterns could ever have been changed. But still . . .

7:30 PM: Well, and here my father says my mother's name. We better go upstairs.

For the last time, Hank and I help them up to their beds, pulling down covers, closing windows, putting on lights. I help my mother undress—again I hug her—but she is preoccupied with a zipper and fumbles unsuccessfully to get out of her skirt. Finally she says, Maybe you better put a garbage bag on the old chaise-lounge, the one she has decided to rest on, in case of an accident.

She is somber but determined. I tell her to wait and that Hank and I will be back with the pills. As I leave the room, I see her staring at the wall, looking at nothing in particular.

At the bottom of the stairs, Hank and I see two suicide letters. My mother's, brief and to the point, is underneath my father's. Neither Hank nor I can figure out when she wrote it. She had to do it in her own time, Hank says. He has left my father waiting, like my mother, in his own bed.

8 PM: In the kitchen, Hank and I work frantically. He never questions his role in helping my parents, nor do I question him about it either. There is no time for talk. However, I suspect that his affection for my father has locked him into staying with him until the end. Even though I don't say so, I am enormously grateful.

We take the phone off the hook and doublelock all the doors. Hank warms applesauce for my father while I dish out ice cream for my mother. Then I pour two diet 7-Ups into plastic glasses, the same glasses I used as a child for orange juice. We do not speak.

There are two trays: on my father's is a glass of water, ten Vesparax to be taken orally, and the applesauce and 7-Up, both sprinkled with the powdered Vesparax. The effect is dreadful. The applesauce turns into cold, lumpy porridge and the 7-Up oozes with what appears to be lava. My mother's tray is similar: water and pills and the same lava-like 7-Up and coffee ice cream that looks like it is interspersed with large grains of sand. *Ugh*, Hank and I say to one another, but we head out of the kitchen. We want to get this over with. You help my mother, I whisper to him at the bottom of the stairs, aware that it is easier to be with my father. Perhaps I want to avoid that final, haunted stare.

No! he says. I can't do that.

I see his point and say OK. I'm carrying my mother's tray, anyway. Make sure they say goodbye, I tell him.

Upstairs I put the tray on a small table—

my mother is still staring at the wall—and I tell her that my father is coming in to say goodbye to her. Perhaps this is when some final words can be exchanged by us all, but my mother nods only slightly, almost indifferently, as if I had just told her that it was going to rain.

Hank leads my father into my mother's room. He is stooping and looks uncomfortable. Hank and I stand aside as he shuffles over to where my mother is sitting. He starts to lean over, and I suspect he will kiss her either on the lips or cheek, whichever my mother (who remains impassive) chooses to give him. He leans toward her, addressing her in the most courtly way—Well, goodbye—and here he says her name—it's been—but before he can reach her, perhaps two inches from her face, he suddenly shrieks and lurches to one side, an expression of sheer agony on his face.

It's his back, his back, Hank says, grabbing my father to keep him from falling over. Bed, bed—my father gasps, and while my mother watches speechlessly, Hank lifts my father's head and shoulders while I carry his torso and legs. Like a 2' by 6' piece of lumber, he is lifted and carried horizontally back to his room, where we place him on his bed. He is ashen with pain and groaning. I realize that he is Hank's responsibility now, and I also realize that we have said our goodbyes during the week.

I rush back to my mother's room. There is a sense of haste now. She looks at me and says nothing. I sit on a chair beside her and ask if she is ready. She answers Yes.

My heart, virtually all my emotions, go out to this woman now as I grasp her wrists and say, I guess you should do this quickly. I have accepted that she intends to die. I can't change that. Knowing that, I also realize that it's important from everything I have newly learned about how to do this that, once we begin, she has to act rapidly. I remember what I have read about people who take barbiturates too slowly and pass out before they finish, ending up as vegetables.

She nods, signalling that she wants me to help her. She cannot properly control her gnarled, arthritic hands. Guide them, she says.

For the first and only time we become a team. She reaches for the ten Vesparax, which she takes three at a time with water. Her swallowing reflexes are good, and this takes no longer than 15 seconds. Ice cream, she says, and I help spoonfeed the grainy mixture from a blue Dalton soup bowl. Her left hand is uncoordinated; her right hand useless. Yet she swallows every mouthful, never once hesitating, always opening her mouth wide and watching the spoon and the dwindling supply of ice cream.

Finally, the bowl is empty.

I can see her head sway a little; the pills are taking effect. A little frantically, grabbing the lava-like 7-Up and a tablespoon, I say—and these will be my last words to her—Remember when I was a little girl and sick and hated my medicine and you made me take it in a big hurry? She nods a drugged nod. Let's pretend that you're me, and we'll get rid of all this medicine, and she nods again, her eyes half-open.

My heart is breaking, I think, because she is so determined. I take the tablespoon heaped with huge gobs of chalky 7-Up and help her thrust tablespoon after tablespoon down her throat. Even in her semi-stupor, she sluggishly swallows until there is no more lava, no more ice cream, no more anything except my mother's face with a Groucho Marx moustache caused by the 7-Up mixture.

Her left hand falls into her lap, still clutching the spoon. Her head falls to the left, her mouth falls open. Then she is still. She is not breathing. I wipe her mouth and stare at her, for how long I don't know. Finally I say: You're a brave woman.

I know she is dying. Over a period of two minutes, maybe more, she breathes involuntarily, four, deep, gasp-like breaths.

Then nothing.

Then: I know she is gone.

I stare at her some more. She looks peaceful, resigned, dignified. I hold her hand and remember a phrase we learned as children: *For in the hour of our death, Jesus is with us, and death is sweet.* I wish I had remembered to say that to her, even if it means nothing to me any more. It might have meant something to her.

Her hand is colder and I pull her night-dress higher around her shoulders. As I do so, the front of her nightdress, her bodice, falls away, exposing her breasts. They are lovely breasts, those of a young girl. I pull the nightdress higher and place the sheet and blanket around her waist. I don't want her to get any colder.

I go out to tell Hank.

Across the hall (as Hank will tell me later), my father lies quietly in his bed for a minute, maybe two. When the pain subsides, he regains his breath, and his composure returns. Is this it? he says to Hank, gesturing to the tray. Hank nods and asks if he is all right. My father says Yes, yes, and then, before reaching for the pills, I can't tell you how grateful I am—we are—to you both. You and (he says my name) have been wonderful.

It's because we love you, Hank says.

My father nods and reaches for the tray, which Hank holds out to him. I'm ready now, my father says.

Taking the pills (These first? he asks; Hank nods), he swallows them two at a time, his hand trembling, not so much out of emotion but out of sheer old age and exhaustion.

Then, he takes the applesauce and literally shovels the mixture down spoonful by spoonful, grimacing as he does so. How do you feel? Hank says, and my father looks up and says Woozy. Then the 7-Up, which he half-drinks, half eats with the spoon. Despite growing drowsiness, he is purposeful, fiercely so.

The spoon, then the glass drop slowly, ever so slowly back down on the tray as my father begins to lose consciousness. This entire procedure has taken ten minutes. Maybe less.

Hank watches as my father's posture slackens; the eyes close, the shoulders droop, the hands rest on the tray on his lap, the head nods slightly to one side. He is dying and I haven't said goodbye, Hank suddenly realizes. He leans over and says in my father's ear loudly, a little insistently, *Goodbye,* and he says my father's name, *Goodbye,* repeating his name, *Safe journey.*

And, with that, with eyes still closed, my father extends his right hand and, in a final, impassioned gesture, clutches Hank's arm, grips it tight, and then goes limp. He dies still holding onto Hank.

Ten minutes later, Hank comes to tell me my father has died. I have left my mother's room at almost exactly the same moment, and we meet in the hall. He's gone—She's dead—we say almost in unison.

They did it, I think to myself. They actually did it.

They did it together.

And they did it right.

I wish the story ended there. I wish I could say that my mother and father were quietly pronounced dead, buried, and that was that. I wish stories like this had simpler endings.

Still, it could have been worse.

After Hank and I meet in the hall, I go in to see my father. A wave of relief—gratitude, really—washes through me as I see him lying there, looking as if he is sleeping.

Deliverance.

All the cliches go through my head: going to one's resting place, passing on, going to one's reward, one's final home. As awful as they are, they fit. My father has *left this world,* and thank heaven for that. His head is bowed, his mouth slightly open, his hands resting at his sides. He and my mother are the first dead people I have ever seen and, to my surprise, I am immensely comforted by what's there.

However, Hank and I must act. He has the presence of mind to take each tray down to the kitchen, rinse the spoons, bowls, and glasses, and put them in the dishwasher. I turn the dishwasher on.

I then phone Dr. Rosenthal's office and he is paged right away. Unexpectedly, I break down as I tell him what has happened. I stammer my name and what my parents have done—they've taken their own lives, they've killed themselves—but he has to ask me twice to repeat myself. He cannot understand.

Finally: My God. I'll be right there. Dial tone.

He arrives in less than twenty minutes.

The next three hours are surreal-like recollections. Rosenthal, shaken, rushes upstairs (it occurs to me later that he may have anticipated a more violent ending—guns or knives), and examines my parents to confirm that they are dead. Hank and I tell him that we had left the house earlier and when we got back, found them dead in their beds. I am crying and shaking. The shock of what has happened hits me.

We go downstairs where Rosenthal calls the coroner, apologizing to both him and us, saying this is a technicality that has to be endured. For some reason, I had not expected this. Suddenly my parents' deaths cease being a private matter and become loomingly official. In a fit of paranoia, I rush to the kitchen and turn off the dishwasher, now in its rinse cycle. Why would two people about to die care about cleaning their dishes? I take my handbag down to the cellar, burying it in the bottom of a trash can. It contains a few Vesparax, nothing else out of the ordinary. Later, I will ponder this strange gesture and never understand it.

Almost simultaneously, the coroner, an Italian who speaks bad English, the police chief—crew-cutted, dressed all in beige, tan topsiders (why do I notice such details?)—and three policemen appear. They leave the lights flashing on on their patrol cars (three, I think). The neighbors, peeking out from behind drapes and window blinds, must be going crazy.

A curious thing: After introducing Hank and me, Dr. Rosenthal greets each of these men with one, non-stop sentence: Yes, he had treated these people knew them extremely well had been told by them they were going to do this that they had been stockpiling drugs and he had been expecting this. I almost expect him to grab the crisp beige lapels of the police chief. He sounds so defensive, so protective; of whom, I'll never know.

Everyone is courteous. Can we look around upstairs? the police chief asks, and I say, Yes, of course, and go into the living room with Hank while the police chief goes up to see my parents. Then I go into the kitchen, make myself a stiff drink, and offer the patrolmen something—anything—but they say no. They are extremely sweet, very solicitous.

Rosenthal is trying to reach my sister, but there is no answer. Finally, the police chief and coroner confer with Rosenthal and leave, although they take the suicide letters with them. This sort of thing is happening more and more often, the police chief says as he leaves, shaking my hand.

Rosenthal prepares to leave, too. I walk him outside. Did you know when you left the house what your parents were going to do? he asks before he gets into his car. *Of course we knew,* I say. I cannot lie to this man.

The three patrolmen wait until the coroner's department, through a funeral home, takes the bodies of my parents away for an autopsy. As I am sitting in the living room, I start to sob. The patrolmen, clearly embarrassed, say they will wait in their patrol cars. During this time Susan calls; a neighbor of my parents was finally able to get through to her, telling her there was some kind of "trouble." Hank explains what has happened and Susan asks him to read the suicide letters over the telephone, which Hank does from copies left behind. She says nothing about coming over.

Eventually, two men appear from the funeral home. I remember only one, wearing a grey sports jacket, black trousers, black wing-tip shoes, and white cotton socks. He flashes a large, diamond ring and smells heavily of scent. We know your parents would want the best funeral service possible, he says in treacle tones. My parents couldn't have cared less, I say neutrally.

I tell them I'll accompany them upstairs as they "prepare" my mother and father. They urge me not to, but I insist. It is not that I dislike or necessarily distrust these men; it is simply that I've promised to see my parents through to the end, and that means the very end.

They go first into my father's room, where they conspicuously remove his watch (would they, I wonder, had I not been there?) and place the body in a metallic grey body bag. Suddenly I say with a clinical pride which surprises me, They haven't vomited and their bowels never voided, as if to remind them that my parents did it *right*. In a funny way, I'm proud of that.

103

The men don't respond. They don't want to look at me. They zip up the bag. My father has disappeared into a sack that looks like the kind of plastic container we used to store our prom dresses in.

They take the bag—vertically—down the stairs. At one point the top half careens over and has to be pushed upright again. It is the top half of my father leaning over, like a burped baby collapsing his head and upper torso over someone's shoulder. The effect is both grotesque and hilarious.

I follow the men to the van, where my father is placed in the back, on the floor. The men are panting and sweating. This is hard work.

We follow the same procedure with my mother. I watch with eagle, possessive eyes. Lift, heave. Up, down. Tuck in. Quickly. Zip, Goodbye, Mother.

She is easier to carry downstairs, out the front door, down the steps, to the waiting van and my waiting father. I follow as, again, the men open the van doors and try to place her beside my father. However, there isn't enough room, one of the men trips, my mother bounces off my father and then, quite literally, lays to rest.

An indecorous ending, that part.

I thank the men. They drive away.

Wordlessly, Hank and I turn off all the lights in the house. For some reason, it feels peaceful, comfortable, restful, not at all eerie. We collapse in bed and fall asleep almost immediately.

We get up at dawn, only four hours later. Almost in total silence, we gather all of my father's correspondence and medication, placing them in plastic garbage bags, drive to a park near the motel where we registered the day before, and dump the bags in trash bins. We then go to the motel and check out.

Susan appears at about nine o'clock. She looks drawn and exhausted, but shows no emotion other than a restiveness which she transforms into a brisk competence. She never once (as Hank points out later) asks any question about our parents, never expresses any curiosity about their dying. Yet she has telephoned everyone and will take charge of all particulars. This seems to console her, as if she needs tasks and chores to keep her from standing still and thinking about what has happened.

Her son, Mark, appears at about ten. There is no affection or demonstrativeness displayed. He is cool and accommodating, polite to me, deferential to his mother. A patrician young man in his last year of college, he regards me with a mixture of aloofness, bemusement, and, I suspect, not entirely flattering interest. I cry intermittently, losing my composure and occasionally my coherence. Whenever this happens, he and Susan look startled and offended, as if I had broken some fundamental rule. Maybe I have.

The Konigs, the neighbors so long absent, come over at ten-thirty, asking if they can "buy" garden shears, carpets, fireplace tongs, and a dropleaf table. My parents have been dead only 15 hours. The Konigs' behavior is so extraordinary that I respond as if I were in the habit of conducting a garage sale for my parents on a daily basis. Later, in looking back, this scenario will strike me as one of the most perverse of all the things that happened.

But there are many unsettling things. In short, Hank and I want to get out of there. Although he doesn't say much, he is feeling the strain too. We are intruders now, wary of Susan, slightly paranoid in the midst of her cool civility. Even Hank, normally nonjudgmental, is a little afraid of her.

After two days of cleaning, organizing, allotting what goes to whom (namely Susan and me, although I want little), Hank and I arrange to fly home the following morning. The coroner has telephoned Monday evening, asking if I have any idea what medication my parents used to end their lives. He is pumping me, I know. In a pique of mischievousness, I tell him that Susan, the primary caretaker, was intimately involved in their care and medication. When I hang up, I laugh heartily.

Dr. Rosenthal calls the following evening, asking the same question. Do you know the pills your parents took to kill themselves? he asks, cordially but a little more formally. I respond by commenting—casually, I think— that I have absolutely no idea. But let me know if you find out, I say to him.

Before he hangs up, he says, a little halt-ingly: I think your parents did the right thing.

I know, I say. I know they did.

Susan makes a brief appearance early Wednesday morning to "check things out" before Hank and I leave. When she says good-bye, I make sure I am in another room. I can-not face her. I want to avoid looking at the same mute distress I saw in my mother for so many years.

The taxi comes, and Hank and I close and lock the door of the house that I still considered home after all these years. I say goodbye to it, to the neighborhood now filled with strangers, to the elementary school whose PTA did not appreciate my mother, to a way of life that will never again be any part of me except in my memories.

I want to go home now. My real home.

I never hear from Susan again. Her son never answers letters I have written him.

God knows what they think of me, I say to Hank.

Of us, he says.

Then: It doesn't matter, he says.

But, deep down, somehow it does matter. Family, like weeds and bad habits, is hard to shake off.

I read somewhere that Pueblo Indians mourn a death for six months and then emerge from their grief with a celebration. The dead have passed to another world, life goes on, and they, the survivors, have reentered it.

Without intending to, I seem to have given myself a year.

On the anniversary of my parents' deaths, unaware at first of the date, I sat down and started writing about them. Once started, I couldn't stop. When I discovered the coincidence of dates, I mused over the timing, probably not at all coincidental. A year was obviously what I needed.

A year was also what Hank and I needed for our marriage to recover. There were still wounds, and, for many months, an inability to draw back and look at each other with anything approaching objectivity. In the end, I came to see him differently than I had at any other time in our marriage and probably he felt the same. Coping with his brother's sudden death drained his emotional reserve; coping with my parents' final illnesses had a similar effect on me. Death was so unnatural that we buttressed ourselves against our own mortality by withdrawing. It was all we knew how to do at the time.

Ultimately, I became aware of the courage and persistence Hank showed in his final week with my mother and father. At the time, I was incapable of seeing that his loyalty to my parents was an integral part of his struggle—often mute—for our marriage. In participating in my parents' chosen way of death, he and I were bonded as surely as if we had participated in some ancient, mystical, and secret rite.

Maybe we did.

I think a lot about my parents, about their curious, last act of bravery and defiance, so uncharacteristic of them.

Yet was it?

For two months after they died, I spend long hours pouring over the albums containing photographs of their parents and grandparents, and dozens—perhaps hundreds—of pictures of them growing up. Everything is organized and systematized until my sister and I are born, when the documentation becomes sloppier. Pictures of us are tied carelessly with rubber bands, often thrust into plain brown envelopes. If there is any identifying commentary on the back, it is always in my father's hand: Avon Beach, 1945; Sarasota, 1953; Susan, aged 9.

Tucked in the backs of albums are letters my father received from friends after college, letters which talk about little except jobs, dating ("Have you had much luck in that department?"), increased rent ("Gee, the landlord is getting greedy. $5 more a month!"). Why would he save such letters? Still, I discover that he was the head of a walking club, that he liked to collect sayings about perseverance, that he kept a separate album of cuttings which followed his brothers' careers, marriages, and childrens' births. *Gloria Bennett born 3 AM Healthy seven pounds.*

My mother's photographs show a slow deterioration, although (with one exception) none—even those of her as a child—radiates gaiety or spontaneity. Even among the gladiolas, she is posed in velvet suits and high-button shoes, fortifying herself for vicissitudes I can only guess at.

There is only one photograph—perhaps she is seventeen—where she sits in a white lace and organdy dress, looking at the camera; she is leaning forward, her gaze direct, unembarrassed; the smile is open and unguarded. It is an exquisite picture, and it stuns me whenever I see it. This is my mother as she should have been, the substance of whatever it was that struggled and lost and which never resurfaced again.

My parents were wonderful people, she said to me in flat tones the afternoon of her death. I no longer know what to believe when I consider the quiet desperation of her life, day after day, year after year.

Through all the photographs and odd memorabilia, I try to grasp who my parents were, yet they elude me. I manage to find a picture of them sitting on a jetty, probably the one on Chesapeake Bay my father talked about the afternoon he died. Yet the photograph shows none of the abandonment or passion my father hinted at. There are two people, they might be unrelated, my father in flannel trousers and a blazer, standing formally behind my mother who sits on a rock looking somewhere else, not at the camera, not at the sea, not at my father.

These are my parents, the two people who, through the most intimate act, conceived me, gave birth to me, raised me. I should know them better, understand them more clearly. I should be able to explain them better.

Yet, in the end, I am the residue of two strangers' lives.

So. We are left with two lives ended, lives that were difficult and not terribly happy, lives which, in large part, were never realized.

Yet my parents' dying was a triumph of sorts. For my father, it was a final statement, an exclamation, a throwback—and a deserved one—to a visionary young man who singlehandedly educated his family and himself, insisting that they deserved something better. One hears that people die the way they live, and it became apparent to me that my parents were drawing on resources that had enabled them to survive long and independently; my father, the logician, carefully assessing every alternative before taking the final, inevitable step. My mother, ultimately giving in to the dependence and, in her own way, the love that she felt for my father.

Still, her death was an astonishing act. Initially she was less clear-headed about it than my father. Although she didn't say so, I know she was not entirely ready to die. During that last week, she silently weighed the few alternatives left and, one by one, realized that none held any appeal for her. She preferred to be with my father. She would not leave Philadelphia, her home for 50 years. She would not go to a nursing home. She would not be helpless, dependent, nor would she be a casualty of old age and protracted dying. Her fate would be the same as her husband's. Once decided, she would not turn back.

Your displays of emotion are appreciated, she said just before she died. In fact, I think they were. She was not alone at the end.

My father's death was his finest hour. He was once again in charge, setting an example, insisting that he and my mother deserved something better than a fate over which they had no control.

We won't endure that, he had said over and over again, and, in the end, he showed us all that he meant it.

And, in the end, for him, at last, the mermaids sang.

II.

Double Suicides and Mercy-killings/Suicides: A Study of 97 Cases

While the deaths of Claudia Lugus's parents may seem an isolated and startling example of double suicide, there were, in fact, three similar cases within the same month and several more before the year ended. Examples: In Walnut Creek, California, an ailing 75-year-old man shot his 74-year-old wife, also ill, before turning the gun on himself. In a suicide letter, the couple noted their failing health and suicide pact.

Another husband and wife in Virginia, both in their sixties, chose to end their lives rather than live with the wife's debilitating illness. Although Mary Jean Crate suffered from blood leukemia, she was expected to live another five years. Her husband, a retired Air Force lieutenant colonel, worked part-time as a real estate agent. "They had a good life together," their son said. "They had each other. I guess my father figured that after 40 years together, he just couldn't see going on without her." Mr. and Mrs. Crate died by carbon monoxide poisoning, using a compact car with the engine running in their garage. They left several notes for family members.

And in Highland Park, Texas, after a 50-year marriage and successful medical careers, Don and Betty Morris could not bear the thought of being separated or of ending their lives in a nursing home. On a warm and humid Monday, the 76-year-old couple indulged in their final meal—scrambled eggs and cheese, bacon, ice cream, and corn chips—all forbidden foods. Afterward, sipping their favorite sherry in their bedroom, they lay in one another's arms, letting the poison they had taken, lethal doses of Nembutal, take effect. "The two of them could function well, but not alone," one of their children said. "If Dad had another heart attack, that would have put Mom in a nursing home. They had seen too many friends who had been placed in nursing homes."

The Morrises left a list of poems reflecting on death, along with a menu of their last meal and several suicide notes. "In the past, everybody used to die too soon," Dr. Morris said in his letter. "Today, the problem of many deteriorating old people is obviously a new one. Therefore, as a society, we have not learned to deal with it in a decent and respectable manner."

Within the next three months there would be seven more cases, either mercy-killings/suicides or double suicides among elderly, ailing couples. In four of these, one of the spouses was terminal and the other in fragile health. In the other three, both the husband and wife were gravely ill.

In four instances, a gun was used. In two, there was a drug overdose. In one, the couple died in their garage with their car engine running. "They were totally dependent on one another, they could not live without one another," a neighbor said of one husband and wife. "And they were a little desperate."

When describing nearly all the couples' relationships, this was a sentiment expressed with alarming regularity.

For several decades, experts have agonized over the rash of youthful suicides. True, the trend has reached epidemic proportions, as the suicide rate for young people between 15 and 24 has risen nearly 300% in the last 25 years.

Yet little if any attention has been paid to what has been happening to our parents and grandparents, many of whom are choosing to take matters into their own hands—overdosing themselves to death, shooting themselves, or poisoning themselves with carbon monoxide fumes. Many, like the above couples, are choosing to do it together rather than endure life alone.

And, indeed, for senior citizens, what does fate hold in store for them as they age? As Lois Martin, 71, wrote to the Hemlock Society shortly before she and her husband took their lives: "Our old people are discards and we're not allowed to make our own decisions. We are captives of our own people. A concentration camp in war could not be any more cruel or less caring for the dignity of the individual than our physicians and lawmakers."

Another couple in their 80s, who shot themselves in the front seat of their car, wrote: "Dear Children, This we know will be a terrible shock and embarrassment. But, as we see it, it is one solution to the problem of growing old."

Growing old—rapidly becoming the ultimate obscenity in a culture obsessed with youth. Instead of a bouncy Grandma baking apple pies beside a wise old grandfather dispensing homilies in the family rocker, the reality of aging is altogether different: Too often, it is a lonely, desperate life, with little to celebrate and much to dread. Like Claudia Lugus' parents, the pattern is much the same: Work and children are gone. Friends have died. Much of the past is lost as memory fails. Painful illness has replaced physical well-being, self-esteem has turned to self-disdain. As one 84-year-old woman commented, "Growing old in America is an unbelievably lonely nightmare. I pray every night I may die in my sleep."

As a result, more elderly people are taking their own lives. Available statistics are worth noting:

• Those older than 60 represent 12%

of the population but commit about 25% of all suicides each year.

• In 1982, suicide was the 14th leading cause of death for people over 65.

• In 1982, those people with the highest suicide rate were in the 75–84 age group. The group with the next highest suicide rate were those people older than 85. Third highest was the 65–74 age group.

• In 1983, elderly white men had a suicide rate of 40.2 per 100,000 people, double the figure for the overall elderly population and triple the rate for the general population. (And in sharp contrast to the 12.1 per 100,000 rate for young people between 15 and 24.)

Yet many experts consider these to be conservative estimates. Statistics ignore the multitudes of old people who simply stop taking their medication or take too much, who drive their cars into trees on lonely stretches of road, or those who deliberately mismanage their diets or whose appetites "disappear." Such instances of so-called "subtle suicide" may be underreported because the cause of death may be less than apparent, or, if it is apparent, because family members are too embarrassed to let it be publicly known.

As one expert commented, "If the official figure is that the elderly commit about a quarter of all reported suicides, I think the true figure is closer to 30 or 40%."

Less than one hundred years ago, life expectancy for the average American was 49 years old. For those over 65, chances were in their favor that they would be living with their children. Most elderly people died at home.

Today, things are different. Life expectancy is 74 years old. An overwhelming majority of people over 65 live with their aged spouses, alone; 15% of these live in poverty, and an estimated 30% in substandard housing. Many of the rest live in nursing homes, where they are patronized and routinely drugged. More than 80% of these people, regardless of where they live, will die in hospitals. Once there, as ethicist Joseph Fletcher puts it, they will probably be "in a sedated or comatose state, betubed nasally, abdominally and intravenously, far more like manipulated objects than moral subjects."

While the wizardry of modern medicine has enabled people to live longer and in many cases better lives, it has also condemned many, like those Fletcher writes of, to a slow, lingering dying, often against their will. People *are* living longer, but in many cases with failing minds and bodies brought on by degenerative diseases which encourages a "dying by inches." As Dr. Robert N. Butler comments in *Why Survive? Being Old in America,* "We have shaped a society which is extremely harsh to live in when one is old." He goes on to say: "The tragedy of old age is not the fact that each of us must grow old and die, but that the process of doing so has been made unnecessarily and at times excrutiatingly painful, humiliating, debilitating, and isolating."

The financial worries of aging don't help either. Not only does Medicare not cover the annual $45,000 to $64,000 cost of a nursing home, neither do private insurance policies. The only thing that does contribute is the Medicaid program, available only if almost all family savings, pension, and other retirement income have been drained or turned over to the government.

On top of that, the average cost of dying is roughly $30,000. More than a quarter of the country's $75 billion yearly Medicare budget is used to maintain the elderly in the last year of life, and most of that during the final month. Thus, not only do old people fear a protracted and painful dying, they fear one that will drain whatever financial resources remain for them and their family.

"Suicide as an option for old people is becoming more and more popular because people are taking control of their fate," observes Vincent Cristafalo, director of the Center for the Study of Aging at the University of Pennsylvania. "Medical technology is such that people can know that they're going to become very ill and that they're going to be in very great pain."

As Dr. Stephen Blum, a gerontologist who has studied American nursing home care for ten years, comments: "Life used to be nasty, brutish, and short. Now, it's nasty, brutish, and long."

For centuries, suicide was regarded by many as a justified, even noble act. In ancient Greece and Rome, many philosophers defended the right to end it all, arguing, as Zeno did, that "intolerable pain, mutilation, or incurable disease" warranted the taking of one's own life. In Athens, magistrates kept a supply of hemlock for anyone who wished to die. Similarly, Seneca argued that "If the body is useless for service, why should one not free the struggling soul? Perhaps one ought to do this a little before the debt [death] is due, lest, when it falls due, he may be unable to perform the act."

Vikings and Scythians considered suicide a virtue when they could no longer continue the nomadic lifestyle they valued in pre-Medieval times, and four suicides are recorded in the Bible. While St. Augustine and St. Thomas Aquinas were prominent Christians denouncing suicide in the 5th and 13th centuries, equally prominent figures surfaced in the 16th, 17th, and 18th centuries, defying church doctrine by claiming, as Sir Thomas More did, that "Since your life's a misery to you, why hesitate to die?" Montaigne held that "The voluntariest death is the fairest," and Francis Bacon insisted that doctors help dying patients "make a fair and easy passage from life."

While there were always dissenters, arguing that preservation of life and God's will were the ultimate virtues, the defense of suicide continued. In the 19th century, Schopenhauer emphasized man's right to the nature of his life and death, and Nietzsche reminded his readers that the thought of suicide was a "strong consolation. . . . one can get through many a bad night with it."

In 1897, French sociologist Emile Durkheim published *Le Suicide*, analyzing suicide as a social phenomenon. He attributed its elevated rate to social, moral, political, and geographical alienation, or "anomie." A few years later, German psychiatrist-philosopher Alfred Hoche coined the term *Bilanz Slebstmord*, or "balance-sheet suicide," citing examples of apparently rational suicide by people who had reviewed their lives, weighed the pros and cons, and decided that, ultimately, death was preferable to life.

By the 20th century, with startling advances in medical technology, a handful of physicians in America and abroad began to argue about "medical euthanasia" as a form of assisted suicide—or the duty of the attending physician, as one doctor put it, to "legalize the termination of absolutely hopeless cases of injury and disease." Prior to World War I, efforts to introduce euthanasia or aid-in-dying bills into state legislatures or British Parliament, however, failed. Typical resistance stemmed from arguments that avaricious or overburdened relatives would too easily rid themselves of an ailing family member, and that confidence in doctors would be undermined. One *New York Times* editorial equated euthanasia with "practices of savages all over the world."

In the following decades, even though suicide was decriminalized, the ethics of it were still hotly debated. Assisted suicide remained a crime, regardless of the circumstances. And, despite the growing number of doctors (and others) bemoaning the fate of dying patients kept alive against their will, attempts to reduce needless suffering through some form of sanctioned euthanasia still led nowhere. With all the blessings of modern medicine, aging threatened to become what Jonathan Swift had so savagely caricatured in *Gulliver's Travels* in the 18th century, writing of the Struldbergs, creatures endowed with immortality.

> At age ninety they lose their teeth and hair; they have at that age no distinction of taste, but eat and drink whatever they will get, without relish or appetite. The diseases they were subject to still continue, without increasing or diminishing. In talking, they forget the common appellation of things, and the names of persons, even of those who are their nearest friends and relations. For the same reasons they can never amuse themselves with reading, because their memory will not serve to carry them from the beginning of a sentence to the end.

To many old people, ironically, modern medicine 200 years later appeared to be creating its own Struldbergs.

Thus, the old and ailing who wished to escape such a fate had recourse to little except their own resources. If the medical establishment and the law were unable to help them, they would take matters into their own hands. A pattern, barely discernible at first, began to emerge which, over eight decades, would persist and eventually multiply with a logarithmic regularity.

In 1911, the Laforgues—he a French writer, she the daughter of Karl Marx—took their lives together. Both were approaching 70. "Before pitiless old age (which is taking from me one by one the pleasures and joys of existence, and depriving me of my intellectual strength) paralyzes my energy, breaks my life, and makes me a burden to myself and others," Laforgue wrote in his final letter, he would kill himself, as he and his wife did. In the next six decades, there were six "mercy-killing" cases in America. In each instance, a family member took the life of a suffering, chronically or terminally ill loved one. In five of the six cases, the deceased had repeatedly begged to be allowed to die.

Other euthanasia-related cases surfaced. "The record of a previously noble life is precisely what makes it sheer insult to allow death in pitiful degradation," wrote feminist Charlotte Perkins Gilman, who, in 1935, killed herself with chloroform at the age of

75. She suffered from cancer. "We may not wish to 'die with our boots on,' but we may well prefer to die with our brains on," she said.

Forty years (and 24 mercy-killing cases, six double suicides) later, in 1975, Henry (Pitney) Van Dusen and his wife, Elizabeth, shared precisely that sentiment. Van Dusen, former president of Union Theological Seminary and a member of the Euthanasia Education Council, and his wife took overdoses of sleeping pills in a suicide pact. "Since Pitney had his stroke five years ago," Elizabeth Van Dusen wrote in a farewell letter to friends and family, "we have not been able to do any of the things we want to do. My arthritis is even worse. There are too many helpless old people who, without modern medicine, would have died, and we feel God would have allowed them to die when their time had come."

Commenting on the Van Dusens' deaths, Norman Cousins wrote that "Death is not the greatest loss in life. The greatest loss is what dies inside us while we live. The unbearable tragedy is to live without dignity or sensitivity."

Eight years later, in 1983, a similar pact was carried out by prize-winning author Arthur Koestler, 77, and his wife, Cynthia, 55. Like the Van Dusens, they killed themselves by taking an overdose of barbiturates. Despite the fact that Cynthia Koestler was in good health, she stated in a suicide note that she could not live without her husband. Koestler, a longtime member of the British Voluntary Euthanasia Society, suffered from Parkinson's disease and leukemia. According to friends he found life "intolerable." "The prospect of falling peacefully, blissfully asleep is not only soothing but can make it positively desirable to quit this pain-racked mortal frame," Koestler wrote. "There is only one prospect worse than being chained to an intolerable existence: the nightmare of a botched attempt to end it."

In the seven-year period between 1980 and 1987, 97 documented cases occurred in America in which both spouses died together—66 mercy-killings/suicides and 31 double suicides. As noted, there were only a half-dozen similar cases in the two previous decades.

Slightly more than half the time, suicide letters were left. Invariably they referred to failing health, fear of hospitals and nursing homes, and financial worries, all curiously reminiscent of Durkheim's "anomie."

Often, too, there was a fear of living without one's mate or of leaving her or him without a proper caretaker. One 71-year-old, who shot his wife and then himself, mentioned in his suicide letter the frustration of welfare cutbacks and of a society that failed to care. "I can't look after my wife any more," the man wrote. "I promised her I wouldn't put her in a nursing home. We don't want to be separated. We'd prefer to go together."

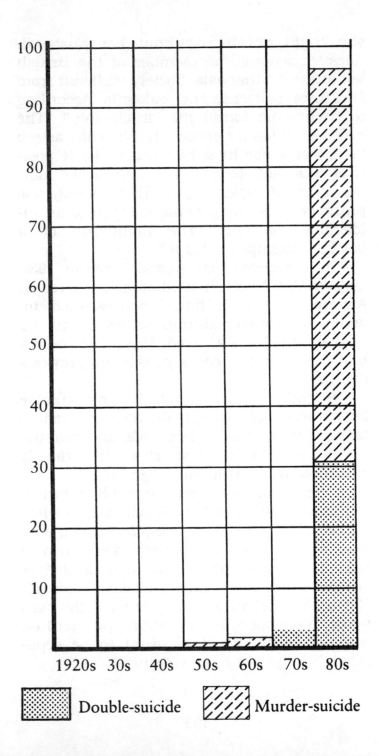

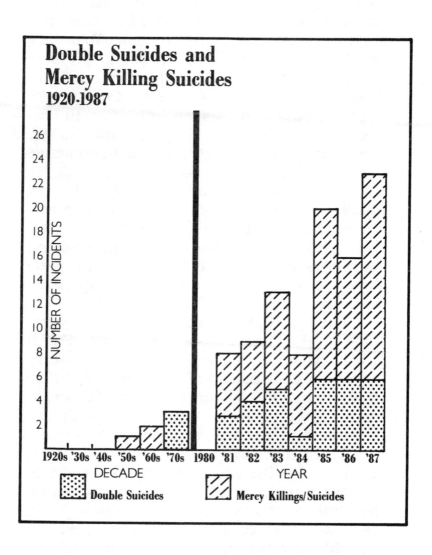

Double Suicides and
Mercy Killing Suicides
1920-1987

Since the 1950s, euthanasia societies in Great Britain and America have been campaigning for the rights of the terminally ill and, intermittently, for physician aid-in-dying. In 1935, the British Voluntary Euthanasia Society was formed to promote "The Voluntary Euthanasia Legalization Bill." Their efforts were unsuccessful. Despite several attempts to pass such legislation in Parliament over the next 50 years, they failed, even though the Society has remained active in upholding patients' rights.

On the other side of the Atlantic, in 1938, the Euthanasia Society of America was formed, modelled after its British counterpart. Repeated attempts to have aid-in-dying bills passed in state legislatures were made over the next thirty years, but few sponsors and little support resulted.

Finally, in the late 1960s, the Society (renamed the Euthanasia Education Fund) withdrew its legislative efforts and concentrated on distribution of the Living Will (formulated in 1969 by attorney Louis Kutner), a patient directive forbidding extraordinary treatment in cases of catastrophic illness.

In the mid-1970s, the group—now called Concern for Dying—concentrated its efforts on distribution of this document, while its political counterpart, Society for the Right to Die, attempted to legalize the Living Will in individual states. By 1987, 37 states and the District of Columbia had adopted some form of Living Will legislation, reinforcing a patient's right to refuse therapy and treatment.

However, as auspicious as this may have

seemed for the dying, the Living Will proved to have fewer teeth than had been hoped. An alarming number of cases surfaced in which patients sued hospitals for treating them against their will, even when they had signed a Living Will and had discussed it with their physician. Hospitals argued that preservation of life surpassed all other priorities, and a significant number of court cases upheld such claims.

Also, the Living Will had little relevance in cases where the illness required more than removal of life supports to provide a much-desired end of life. In many instances, old age, fragility, and a series of deteriorating illnesses made "pulling the plug" simplistic and not the answer. Not surprisingly, then, of 79 mercy-killing cases that took place between 1970 and 1985, three out of four occurred in states with Living Will legislation. Of mercy-killings/suicides or double suicides, more than 90% took place in such states.

A typical case is that of a 73-year-old couple in Kansas, who wrote their obituaries and paid for their funerals before taking their lives. Both were suffering from emphysema and heart ailments and did not want to live in a nursing home or hospital. "What is left?" Martha Helmstead told her husband's cousin the day before she died. Any further treatment would be costly, intricate, cumbersome, and, for the Helmsteads, unwanted.

"We have completely run out of energy," Walter Helmstead wrote in his suicide note. Whatever Living Will legislation existed would be meaningless, any withholding of life supports purposeless. The couple had approached the "line of unbearability" Dr. Marv Miller speaks of in *Suicide After Sixty: The Final Alternative*, "the point where the quality of our lives [is] so pathetically poor we no longer wish to live."

Double Suicides and Mercy-killings/Suicides: Statistics and Examples

In August 1980, in response to the growing demand for physician aid-in-dying, the Hemlock Society was formed in Los Angeles, California. Its ultimate aim? To educate lay people and health-care workers so that right-to-die legislation would pass in at least one of the states. This legislation would enable a terminally ill person to have his dying accelerated—if he or she requests it and if the physician is willing to perform the act. As one supporter wrote, "Pulling the plug just isn't the answer in most cases. Dying is so much more complicated. Medical technology has made sure of that. Most of us die from more than one thing, and withholding or withdrawing treatment is only one-tenth of the issue, if that. We deserve the right to choose, to have us put out of our misery, if that's what we want."

In the seven years before such legislation was formulated, Hemlock published manuals for the dying, distributed Living Will and Durable Power of Attorney documents, and held annual conferences to discuss right-to-die issues. It also amassed statistics on the number of mercy-killing cases in America, as well as suicides due to terminal illness, assisted suicides, and double suicides or mercy-killings/suicides in which terminal or chronic illness was a factor.

Figures were alarming. In the 60-year period between 1920 and 1980, there were 41 reported euthanasia-related cases (mercy killings, autoeuthanasia/suicide, mercy-killings/suicides, and double suicides). In the seven-year period between 1980 and 1987, there were 139 documented cases. While it can be assumed that many suicides and attempted suicides were not reported in the previous decades, the contrast is still startling.

With simultaneous deaths, as stated, the rate jumped to ten times what it had previously been (double suicides) and in mercy-killings/suicides, more than twenty times what had existed in the three-decade period prior to 1980. While these figures are estimates at best, they represent a trend which cannot be ignored.

If such deaths are underreported, one wonders how much more alarming more precise statistics might be. As it is, figures show that euthanasia-related cases can be broken down in the following way:

Mercy-killings/Suicides:

While there is no typical profile for the

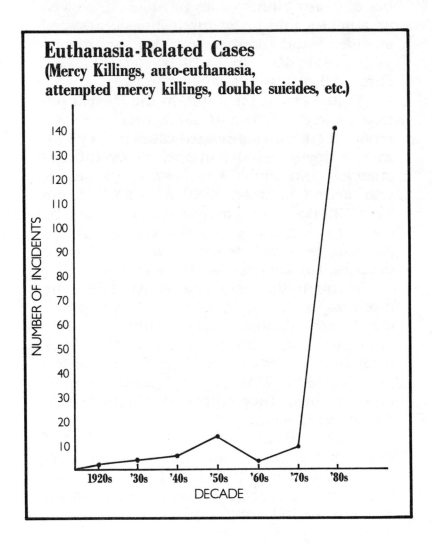

Euthanasia-Related Cases
(Mercy Killings, auto-euthanasia,
attempted mercy killings, double suicides, etc.)

couple who ends their lives this way, the chances are two out of three that either the wife will be the sole sufferer or that she and her husband will be gravely ill; in other words, in only a small percentage of cases is the husband the sole ailing spouse, even though most of the time he will be the instigator. Also, a gun will be used. If there is a pet, it will be put to death along with the married couple. None of these people, if they have children, will live with them. A note will probably have been left behind. Exhaustion, helplessness, fear of parting, poor prognoses, and fear of institutionalization are invariably cited as factors.

In the case of Charles and Joyce Bowen, he 97, she 80, coping mechanisms had failed. Few, if any, acceptable alternatives remained. "My wife is very sick and I can't walk any more," Bowen told a neighbor the day before they died. A retired commercial artist, he suffered from a heart ailment, his wife from cancer. After calling a friend in Connecticut to tell them he and his wife had to decided to end it all, Bowen shot his wife in the head and then himself. "They were as devoted as a couple can get," a neighbor later said. "If he did it, it was because of his devotion to her."

Fear of leaving a mate can be a powerful motive, exacerbated by fear of nursing homes or extended hospital stays for the surviving spouse. "I'm afraid with all the strain that someday I might have an attack and leave my wife, and that is something I cannot do," 88-year-old Leslie Hypes noted in a tape record ing left behind after taking the lives of his wife and himself. "I do not want to live without her," he said, referring to his 87-year-old wife, Elsie. Both had serious health problems; Elsie Hypes was blind and she and her husband were partially bedridden and increasingly unable to care for one another. She had pleaded with her husband not to commit her to an institution. "Elsie is so helpless, and I cannot [leave her], and, if God will forgive me, it is the best way out," Hypes said in the recording.

In more than 10% of the deaths, one spouse was in a nursing home or was temporarily hospitalized, and in every instance it was the wife. In every case but one a gun was used. The husband, allotted the role of caretaker, was functional although increasingly feeble and unable to accept his wife's suffering. Fear of separation made the situation even more intolerable. For example, in Park Ridge, Illinois, 82-year-old Milton Pollock, a retired sanitation department worker, shot his 82-year-old wife, who was temporarily hospitalized. He then shot himself. "He was terrified," a good friend said, who had talked to Pollock before he left for the hospital. "He said he didn't know how he could handle it if he had to put his wife in a home."

Loren Eve's sentiments were similar: "I have watched this beautiful lady Helen, my wife, whose heart and Christian soul are even more beautiful, go downhill for quite some time. But her suffering this past year has become more intense and to the point of being almost unbearable." Eves was 80, his wife 73, and in and out of hospitals for years. In the case of Harry and Lydia Miller, both in their eighties, Miller's deteriorating health prevented him from looking after his wife. "He couldn't take care of her," a friend commented. "He knew she would never come back." In both sets of deaths, a gun was used. All four died instantly.

A similar pattern surfaced in cases where, again, it was the wife who was institutionalized with the husband designated caretaker. Once again, a gun was used to end their lives (with one exception, where the couple died from carbon monoxide poisoning). However, in this cluster—here, 15%—the wife suffered from Alzheimer's or advanced senility.

Precipitating factors were invariably the same as in the above-noted deaths, where fear of prolonged institutionalization and pain of separation ranked high. Just before Denby Coon shot his wife of 42 years and then himself, for example, he wrote to friends that he had been unsuccessful in finding the right kind of nursing home where he and his wife could receive the care he felt they deserved. Coon, a retired postal worker, had been looking after his elderly wife whose mind, friends said, was "wasted."

In the case of Fred and Margaret Curry, financial worries were cited as a contributing cause. Curry, 85, fatally shot his 73-year-old wife with a .45-caliber handgun in St. Anthony's Convalescent Center in Houston, Texas, before shooting himself.

In Atlanta, Georgia, Raymond Frechette took his wife from a convalescent residence home for an evening, ostensibly to celebrate her 85th birthday. After giving his wife a birthday card, however, Frechette killed her with a shotgun blast before turning the gun on himself. A note he left in the kitchen was headed "The Cause is Alzheimer's." In it, Frechette said he wondered who would care for his wife if he died before she did.

And in Missola, Montana, Asberry Smith, 79, told investigators that he fully intended to die of carbon monoxide poisoning with his wife, Laurlee, who also suffered from Alzheimer's. The couple started their pickup truck, running a hose from the exhaust pipe into the canopied rear bed. While waiting for the poisonous gas to fill the truck, Smith got out to adjust a high-idling choke and passed out on the ground behind the vehicle. He survived the suicide attempt, his wife did not.

In court, where Smith was charged with mitigated homicide, Deputy County Attorney Ed McLean testified that for days before her death, Laurlee Smith had begged her husband to end her suffering. Later, after the suicide attempt, McLean testified that "When I asked Smith in the hospital why he wanted to die, he said life wouldn't be worth living without her."

"Did you do what you did, as far as you're concerned, under extreme emotional or mental stress?" the judge asked Stern.

"I would think so," Smith responded.

In only four reported cases did the wife take the initiative in causing death, and here a gun was used. Typical of these were Kathryn and Al Howse who, at 78, were worried about their failing health. After many years as a furniture dealer in Witchita, Howse was a semi-invalid, his wife a heart attack victim with a failing memory. Friends testified to an extremely close-knit, devoted marriage in which Al was very much the boss. However, in the last years of their lives, as health problems worsened, the Howses became virtual hermits. One day, not long after her 78th birthday, Kathryn went to The Bullet Shop where, complaining about the threat of burglars, she purchased a .38-caliber Smith & Wesson revolver for $149.50.

That evening, after she had talked to friends on the telephone, sounding "absolutely normal," she put on a pair of white pajamas and inserted a pair of blue ear plugs. She then held the revolver against the head of the man she had been married to for more than 58 years, firing two bullets into his brain as he lay asleep. Afterward, she walked to the bathroom where, placing the pistol tip against her right temple, she pulled the trigger.

Friends and neighbors later suggested that dying together must have been Al Howse's idea, while others speculated that he never would have allowed such a tragedy. Whatever the case, in the note Kathryn Howse left behind, she said that she and her husband were getting older and were no longer able to care for one another.

Terminal or Ill Spouse
In Mercy Killings/Suicides

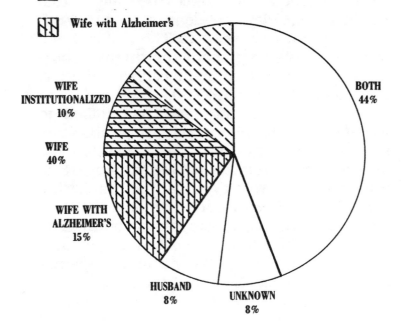

Wife

Wife Institutionalized

Wife with Alzheimer's

WIFE
INSTITUTIONALIZED
10%

WIFE
40%

WIFE WITH
ALZHEIMER'S
15%

BOTH
44%

HUSBAND
8%

UNKNOWN
8%

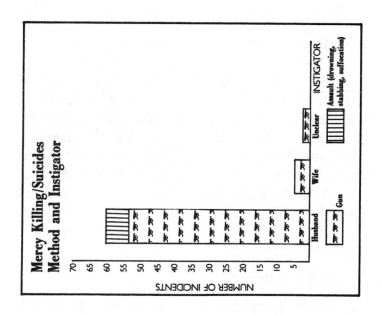

Mercy Killing/Suicides
Method and Instigator

Terminal or Ill Spouse
In Double Suicides

In McLean, Virginia, a nationally-known science fiction writer who was, apparently, despondent over her husband's poor health shot him in the head and then turned the gun on herself. "He was an invalid and she was upset," a police spokesman said of Alice Sheldon, 71, and her husband Huntington, 84. "She didn't want to see him suffer." Only a few years earlier Mrs. Sheldon had written to a friend: "I had always meant to take myself off the scene gracefully about now while I'm still me. And now I find I can't, because that would mean leaving him alone . . ."

In these cases, there was a reversal of the usual pattern: Here the husband was the sicker of the two, with the wife instrumental in carrying out the death pact, if there was one. Yet there is also the suggestion that, notwithstanding the wife's pivotal role, in at least two of the four cases the husband may have been the primary persuader in convincing them to end it all. With Albert and Annie Hilton of Pleasant Grove, Texas, friends commented on Mr. Hilton's headstrong nature. "He probably convinced her to shoot them both," one said, which Mrs. Hilton had done. In all four marriages, the wife had had intensely difficult caretaking responsibilities during the final years of their lives together.

Double Suicides:

When a couple chooses to die, invariably by carbon monoxide poisoning or by a drug overdose, because both methods involve mutual cooperation, the decision is obviously a shared one. While one partner may be the initiator, as observed in some of the above cases, the desire, as one couple wrote, to "continue their journey together" is a powerful motive. Notes and letters attest to this. "We have led full and fruitful lives," a Boston man wrote, "but now that we are both in failing health, we choose to die together in a peaceful and dignified way, something we had planned for several years but denied us by recent medical problems."

The breakdown of which partner is gravely ill is similar to the pattern found when a gun is used. With double suicides, in roughly half the cases, both spouses were ailing; in one-third, the wife was the primary sufferer, and in only five (19%), the husband. (In two cases, it is not known who is the sufferer.)

Such a pattern shows that even when the husband initiates or encourages dying together, in at least one out of three cases, the wife is the sole sufferer. Such a pattern—men following their wives to the grave—suggests several things in both double suicides and mercy-killings/suicides: Not only are men prone to a fear of separation, they appear to have fewer resources as they age, having experienced something of an "emotional fall" after retirement.

No longer working, they become more socially isolated as well as increasingly dependent on their wives. Certainly previously-cited figures reinforce this notion: i.e., that the suicide rate for elderly white males is double that for the overall elderly population and triple the rate for the general population.

Perhaps it's not surprising, then, that so many men are willing to end their lives, despite relatively stable health. Also of interest is the fact that of the 14 couples who committed double suicide with only one ailing spouse, seven had no children.

Whether choosing carbon monoxide poisoning or a drug overdose, in the twelve incidents where both partners were gravely ill, their deaths were, without exception, meticulously planned. They also took place in familiar surroundings: Each couple had their own home or apartment, where they had lived for a long period of time. Every couple but one left a note. In many cases, the note was a lengthy letter or letters.

Typical well-organized planning was demonstrated by Eric and Lotte Synder, in their 80s, of Palo Alto, California. The Synders were blind and in fragile health. Married for nearly 50 years, Synder, a famed research scientist in his field, and his wife were found seated on their sofa, embracing. Empty water glasses and an empty prescription bottle that once held 100 phenobarbital tablets were found on the coffee table in front of them. "They left all kinds of notes," a friend said. "Near them were stacks of packages and boxes of borrowed books with instructions to return them to people. There was even a note for the coroner, identifying the type of drug they took. They left a note for just about everybody but the police." Friends and neighbors said that the Synders had shown no signs of despondency in the weeks prior to their dying.

Other double suicides were consistently described as "well planned," "thoughtful," and "extremely well organized." Several couples who died from carbon monoxide had their pet dogs or cats propped beside them in the car, resting on blankets and cushions as they passed out from the fumes. In almost all cases, in the weeks beforehand there was less apparent despondency, suggesting a mutual empathy and support as well as the kind of resolve evidenced in the deaths of the Synders. In at least six of the twelve cases, couples were either members of the Hemlock Society (mentioned in obituaries) or had been outspoken with family and friends about a person's right to avoid a painful, protracted dying.

For instance, Mary Hopkins wrote in her suicide letter:

> We ask whoever finds us, please do not try to bring us back. We are both old and sick. King is dying of cancer, and I have been ill for a long time. I can no longer live with this cruelty. I am in pain much of the time and my eyesight is failing rapidly.
>
> We have thought about this long and seriously. Our life has been wonderfully happy and satisfying, and we want very

much to die and be remembered by our family and friends as full human beings. . . . Do let us go gentle into that good night.

The Hopkins died from a combination of Seconals and alcohol. "They had apparently decided quite a while ago," a relative said. "They planned it well."

Another man, 86-year-old Whittier Spaulding, had written the following letter to family and friends three years before he and his wife died.

There may come a time in the life of either of us when our senses may be impaired or our minds affected so that we can no longer have control of our own acts or desires. At such time, we have agreed between us that the other shall take it upon him or herself, with the full prior consent and pleading of the other, to take such action as will assure prompt death with dignity to both of us simultaneously.

We have both lived a full, active life, participating in many religious, cultural, and business activities. . . . We believe we have—both of us—contributed much to many aspects of our society and in many places. . . . Now, with our respective disabilities and weaknesses, we are no longer able to make such contributions, but must from now on live on pension and other incomes—consuming assets, services, and resources which can be of greater worth to others.

Why then should we—or others in similar circumstances—demand, require, or be supplied with attentions and services to maintain a dying limb on a tree that can never again produce or render a service to society?

We are aware that society will unlikely come to grips with the problem in our lifetime. . . . However, the world cannot forever provide for an ever-growing number of the elderly, many of whom rapidly reach senility and become totally comatose.

Three years later, as failing health made life too burdensome for them, the Spauldings agreed, as they noted in their final letter, that "this morning we reached a point where we must say goodbye." Beth Spaulding had had two falls and her husband was too fragile to help her. Physical and mental well-being was gone. It was time to die.

Finally, in San Mateo, California, in early 1988, patient advocate Dr. Louis Shattuck Baer, 73, and his wife, Evelyn, 69, were found dead in an apartment they had rented especially for that purpose. The couple had been longtime residents of nearby Burlingame, where Baer practiced medicine. He catered primarily to the elderly. In 1979, he wrote *Let the Patient Decide*, in which he stressed the importance of avoiding painfully drawn-out deaths in nursing homes. A prominent spokesman for the right to die, Baer had argued that "It should be considered good medical practice to let this type of patient die a natural death when infection or heart failure comes as their friend."

Both Baer and his wife had been in ill health; she suffered from terminal cancer. According to friends, they both believed strongly that they did not want to be a burden to anyone in their later years, and they made sure their two grown children knew how they felt. Baer had written extensively about the horrors of nursing homes and protracted dying. "In my type of practice," he commented a few years before his death, "I spend a lot of time making rounds in nursing homes. It brings it all very close to you. I've seen a great deal of the end of life."

Knowing what he knew, aware of the few (if any) acceptable alternatives left for him and his wife, it's possible Baer felt that dying with his wife was better than being victimized by the "system" he had so often warned patients about. By all accounts, the Baers were still very much in love and had worked together for many years. Married 51 years, they were found locked in each other's arms on the couch after taking a drug overdose.

Doubtless, separation would have deprived them of much the substance of their lives. As Baer had written earlier: "Human life is composed of the body, mind, and spirit. Without any of these, it isn't actual living. It's existence. Few of us would agree that that's enough."

What Does it Mean?

Suicide in movies and literature has not been ignored.

In the 1973 movie *Soylent Green*, Edward G. Robinson, portraying an elderly, ailing man whose work is finished, checks into a suicide clinic. Accompanied by two aides, he lies down on a cot in a special chamber where, surrounded by his favorite music and colors, he dies a serene, nearly idyllic death. "I'm going home," he says in a final note to a friend.

Author Kurt Vonnegut Jr., in *Welcome to the Monkey House*, created Federal Ethical Suicide Parlors, where the growing problem of overpopulation was resolved by encouraging senior citizens to receive lethal injections after a final meal catered by Howard Johnson's. In both *Monkey House* and *Soylent Green*, what was presented as satire and science fiction struck many people as eminently sensible. Indeed, Alfred Nobel, founder of the Nobel Prize and the inventor of dynamite, envisioned a "suicide institute" on the Riviera, in which clientele could die in style with a first-class orchestra bidding them goodbye.

New York artist Jo Roman, in *Exit House*, published after her death by an overdose in 1979, planned a suicide center where people could choose from Exit Liquids, Injections, Pills, or Exit Vapor Injections, and then be buried in the Rational Death Woods.

For many people, such ideas are not absurd; they make sense. Yet controversy rages. Suicide prevention workers insist that most suicides, whether single or double, are cries for help; they should be prevented at all costs. Physicians argue that pain can be controlled and that people who are ill will always have access to medication that relieves suffering. To collude in helping someone die is not only unethical, they hold, it betrays the trust between patient and doctor as life-saver and life-sustainer.

Hospice workers claim that their facilities and out-patient care are adequate to provide for the needs of the dying. Others argue that dignifying the suicide argument is part of the "slippery slope" in which, because they are more "burdensome" and their upkeep costly, elderly people will be increasingly nudged into the grave before their time. Some even suggest that such a trend will lead to the Nazi "thrift euthanasia" program in which it is economically expedient to eliminate *all* unproductive members of society: the mentally ill, the handicapped, the ailing, and the old.

Certainly many of the letters left behind by couples who died together make no attempt to conceal frustration and rage over their helplessness and lack of resources. Society is saying, not so subtly, that they are no longer desirable or productive citizens. "Impotent, invalidated, useless, victimized, and dependent," one woman wrote in her farewell note, describing how she and her husband felt before they took their own lives.

Indignation over cutbacks in Medicare and Medicaid are often mentioned, too. In one case, a couple in their 70s suffering from emphysema and a heart ailment received $600 a month from Social Security. After their house payments, utilities, and medical bills, there was $25 left for food. "I'll tell you what killed them," a stepson said. "The government cut back all their money. It didn't take courage to pull the trigger. It took pain."

Others lament the lack of acceptable nursing homes or retirement residences. "We refuse to be infantilized, sedated, and rendered utterly helpless," one husband and wife wrote before taking an overdose of barbiturates combined with alcohol.

Is a significant number of simultaneous deaths, then, a cry for help?

Mercy-killings/suicides: Male-oriented?

In nearly half the cases, as noted, where only one spouse is ill (usually the wife) it is the husband who holds the gun to her head or heart and then to his own. In 40% of these cases, a suicide letter is left behind. In most of these frustration and desperation are mentioned. "I can't look after her any more," one man commented. Another: "My wife is terribly ill and I am too feeble to leave the house." And another: "There's no hope left for Virginia. That's it."

Despondency and urgency characterize not only the tone of many of these notes, but also the manner in which the couple died, whether or not a letter was left. No one would disagree that shooting one's mate and then oneself is anything less than traumatic. So, too, depression and a certain franticness have often been observed in the weeks or months preceding the couple's death, according to friends and neighbors.

Several explanations are possible: As seen, the "functioning" spouse, usually the husband, cannot bear his wife's suffering, nor can he bear the thought of life without her. He may also fear that if something happens to him, she will have no one left to care for her. Finally, unable to endure any more, he takes matters into his own hands. Pills are unavailable or impractical. Stabbing is violent and repulsive. A gun will have to do.

The startlingly high rate of suicide among elderly white males lends support to this argument: This group copes the worst when confronted with loss of employment, loneliness, reduced finances, and potential loss of spouse. (In contrast, elderly males in ethnic minorities are not only more integrated into extended families, but have had to cope most of their lives with alienation and hardship. This, ironically, toughens them for the vicissitudes of old age, experts say.)

Because a third of the total number of cases consisted of a gravely-ill wife and a functioning husband in which the husband took both lives, there is the suggestion of domination that unsettles many researchers. "The line between a love-pact suicide and a murder-suicide can become a fine one," writes Herbert Hendin in *Suicide in America*. "The suicide pact is in fact often a form of tyranny, affirming one partner's desire to control the life of the other." Indeed, is the trend male-dominated?

If this is so, such a pattern might just as easily apply where the husband was terminal and the wife still functioning, yet the two died together. Certainly whatever evidence there is points to heightened dependency with the male as the focal point. With Andrew and Britta Solberg, 67 and 68, it was a matter of not being able to live without the other. "Britta told me 'If you go, I want to go,' " Solberg said to a friend before shooting himself and his wife. Friends commented that Britta feared loneliness without her husband, who had pancreatic cancer.

Similarly, friends and neighbors of Robert and Evelyn Van Horn speculated that Mr. Van Horn had been distraught over his protracted and painful illness for a long time before shooting himself and his wife. "It looks like he was depressed," one friend said. "He wanted to take his life, and he decided to take hers as well." Both Van Horns were 83.

Regardless of which spouse is the primary sufferer, Dr. Milton Rosenbaum would probably support a theory of male "initiation." Distinguished visiting professor of psychiatry at Marshall University School of Medicine in Huntington, West Virginia, he has commented that, in simultaneous deaths, "Suicide pacts are usually not by mutual consent. The man is usually the instigator, and he usually talks his wife into it. Often the wife is reluctant. Often the man is depressed."

Indeed, it's possible that in marriages where one spouse must function as principal caretaker, the partner responsible for feeding, nursing, housekeeping, and shopping becomes so overburdened that he (or, less frequently, she) emotionally and physically short-circuits. Psychiatrist Carl Eisdorfer, in *Loss of Self*, points out that in slightly more than half the cases he studied, the chief caregiver was clinically depressed. "That brings sleep problems, appetite problems, that in turn lead to judgment problems," Eisdorfer wrote. "The future is grim, dark, and dreary, and the judgment is impaired." Violence can follow, he said.

Although the study was concerned primarily with Alzheimer's cases, the syndrome could apply just as easily to anyone caring for long-suffering terminally and chronically ill partners. That factor, and the "tyranny" element, might help explain the high proportion of cases in which the husband, still relatively healthy, shoots his ailing wife and then himself.

Still, another factor may prevail in which the "male-domination" factor is absent. Undoubtedly, in some cases, the gravely-ill wife asks to be killed because she cannot do it herself. While her death is technically recorded as a homicide, it is virtually self-inflicted.

However, the husband, in granting her request, is aware that he faces legal consequences and, thus, in another desperate act, shoots himself. Almost everyone is aware of the widely-publicized Roswell Gilbert case in 1985 in Florida, in which Gilbert was convicted of the first-degree murder of his wife, Emily, who suffered from Alzheimer's disease and osteoporosis. Gilbert, now 79, is serving a 25-year jail sentence. To avoid a similar fate, as well as endure a lonely and isolated life without one's long-term mate, a healthy husband might decide that the best fate is simply to die with his wife. The Gilbert trial is not unique in resulting in prosecution—long, traumatic, and expensive—following a mercy killing.

As Gilbert commented during the trial, "I should have died with Emily."

Double Suicides: A Shared, Class-oriented Decision?

When both partners die together, the pattern changes. Not only is there less impulsiveness and despondency, there is a greater chance that the couple (especially if both are ill) comes from the upper-middle class.

Also, there is more apparent "closure"; aside from the meticulous planning and lengthier letters left behind, in several cases husbands and wives shared their decision-making with family members before they died, even asking some relatives for cooperation.

With mercy-killings/suicides, perhaps because of shame or embarrassment, family members, neighbors, and friends were usually reluctant to reveal much about the deceased. Yet certain comparisons can be made. For instance, in 30 of 66 mercy-killings/suicides, the husband's profession was listed. In more than half of these, husbands had worked the greater part of their adult lives in a "non-professional" capacity: tugboat captain, factory worker, sanitation department worker, mailman, construction worker, or, Fuller Brush salesman. The others had more elevated positions such as geologist, veterinarian, lumber executive, electrical engineer, school principal, or newspaper publisher.

In contrast, with double suicides there was a greater concentration of professional men and, in a few cases, career wives. If there was a drug overdose, the more educated and affluent undoubtedly had better access to barbiturates and were shrewder in stockpiling them. Thus, the possible increase in the relationship between drug deaths and socioeconomic status. Certainly more information was available about these couples, probably because they were more prominent in the community.

Of these double suicides, 21 occupations were listed for the husbands, three-quarters of which were highly-qualified professions. Also, the number of non-professional men increased slightly when only one partner was the primary sufferer. In other words, when both husband and wife were in grave health, it's possible that women married to men in upper-echelon jobs were more likely to participate in the ultimate decision-making.

However, more figures and documentation are needed to confirm this possibility. Still, where both husband and wife had careers and both were ill, the decision to die together in a well-planned way is very much in evidence.

With the double suicides, breakdown of husbands' occupations is listed below. (All were retired.) If the wife had a profession, it is listed beside her husband's.

Husband Primary Sufferer	Wife Primary Sufferer	Both Partners Gravely Ill
Linotype operator	Shipyard worker	Tuxedo manufacturer
Police officer	Maintenance	Investment counsellor
Librarian	worker	Physician
Physician	Pattern-maker	Bank president
	Translator	Company president
	Lt. Colonel	Research scientist/
	(Air Force)	book binder
	Minister	Bank vice-president
	Physician	executive secretary
		College president/
		psychologist
		Psychiatrist/psychologist

Also, when one spouse was ill, slightly more than half the couples left notes and letters. (The pattern was similar, if a little less, in mercy-killings/suicides—40%.)

However, in double suicide cases where *both* husband and wife were ailing, 11 out of 12 couples left notes behind (92%), compared with 55% in mercy-killings/suicides. Higher literacy, less apparent despondency, and greater advance planning might explain this communicativeness. Also, organizing well ahead of time may have given the couple a chance to grieve openly with one another as well as experience mutual relief that there was, at last, not only a way out, but one that they could share together.

It was stated earlier that several couples had written about or discussed their right to die months or years before they did. Such a move suggests a supportive circle of family and close friends; one that is willing to listen and remain nonjudgmental about such a serious decision. In four known cases, in which both husband and wife were in failing health, parents shared their specific intentions to die with sons and daughters within a few weeks of their deaths and requested some form of cooperation. As was the case of Claudia Lugus and others, it's difficult for a family member to accept and facilitate such a move. However, once made, it encourages the kind of peace-making and unity that she spoke of when, in the end, she and her parents became "family."

Diane Callahan speaks of her struggle with her parents' intentions and her final acceptance:

> I started thinking about something I teach my students in psychology class. Individuation. That people own themselves and that you must allow them to make their own choices. My parents weren't Catholics. My father was a Chris-

tian Scientist and my mother was a Mormon, and neither of them was very religious. From their point of view, staying alive was not prolonging their living but prolonging their dying. It took me a lot of struggling, but I finally decided that I had to stop judging them by my values and try to understand theirs instead.

Soon after that, she told her parents that she was willing to support their decision to die together so long as they did not resort to violent means. There was enormous relief on all sides. "When I finally told [my mother] I understood how she felt, we kind of made our peace. [My father] and I got to the depths first. We didn't have time not to."

Later, after her parents had died, Diane visited them in the mortuary.

I started thinking about the strength it took, when they were so weak, to do the research [about the drug overdoses] and fake everyone out on the last night and get out the towels. . . . to muster up, to do the deed, be clever, be sharp, use those brains! . . . I felt especially proud of my mother. . . . I felt, All right [Mom]! So I started talking to them. I said, You were really good parents, and I'm sorry you had to go through so much. And then I said, Hey, you guys. Good job.

With the Martins and other couples, the marriages had been far from ideal. Yet, as sons and daughters came to recognize, a bonding and dependence existed in each relationship that made life without the other partner impossible. Realizing this, it was easier for grown children to accept their parents' decision, as wrenching as it was.

As one son commented, "My parents told me months before what they intended to do. When it happened, I wasn't devastated because I had participated in it. In looking back, I appreciate that they shared their intentions with me. It was better I was a part of it." He then added: "And of course I realized the most important thing of all—my parents couldn't live without each other."

Undoubtedly this is true of many other couples, whether they died in mercy-killings/suicides or double suicides. After their deaths, many husbands and wives were described as extremely reliant on one another with few, if any, outside resources. These were people who had lived together for so long in such powerfully binding, symbiotic relationships that they could not envision survival on their own and did not choose to. As one husband and wife wrote, "We choose to go together while we still know what we're doing. We've had the finest life together imaginable. In the end, we choose to take the scenic route. And, as always, together."

An Overview:

Still, dying together should not be romanticized. Too much agony, frustration, and suffering are apparent in too many of these cases. There is sufficient evidence, especially in mercy-killings/suicides, to suggest overwhelming despair and hopelessness; couples feel that they have no choice but to kill themselves with whatever means are there, regardless of how unsettling these methods are.

Until better resources—not least of which are health-care costs and medical benefits—are improved for the elderly, the picture remains gloomy. For instance, from 1948 to 1981, with improvements in medical care and pension plans, the suicide rate for older people was reduced by nearly half. However, after 1981, with significant cutbacks in medical and welfare benefits, the rate began to escalate and has continued to do so, both with single and double suicides.

In the future, health-care workers should learn to recognize and respond to signs of desperation: Studies show that 75% of all elderly suicide victims visit a doctor within three months before they end their lives. Yet only 3% of calls to suicide prevention centers come from those over 65, reinforcing the notion that not only did adults of this age grow up in an era when it was unacceptable to seek mental-health care, it was a time when the male "lead" was more easily adhered to. And, in contrast to 200 failed attempts for every successful one among adolescents, more than one-quarter of the elderly who attempt to kill themselves—the majority of whom are men—succeed.

Equally important, more money and effort must be put into creating better resources for the aging: upgrading the quality of nursing homes, producing more retirement communities and intermediate-care facilities, as well as making home health care workable for those who want to stay there. Greater emphasis should be placed on developing new spheres of friends for the lonely, decreasing social isolation while affirming a greater feeling of usefulness. Gender-oriented programs might help, too, since the strains of aging appear to have been better tolerated by women than men to date. Perhaps women, like minority men, have been better conditioned to withstand the hardships of aging because of decades of discrimination. Only time will tell.

Until better measures are taken, the specter of spiralling suicides among the old and ailing will rise to near-epidemic proportions: By 2020, when the baby boom generation reaches retirement, there will be 51.4 million Americans over the age of 65, double what there is today.

And, instead of a ratio of one elderly person for every five between 18 and 64, the ratio will have shrunk to one to three. In a word, there will be fewer people available to help support our senior citizen population.

Even if all these criteria were filled, however, would this still be enough? Medical advances will continue to enable people to live longer, but with an even greater number of spun-out illnesses and degenerative diseases. The Struldbergs threaten to proliferate. What of the right to die, of those who, with or without a spouse, refuse to endure such a fate?

Many people still see suicide as an honorable option, one embodied in the Greek and Roman ideal of a noble death. And many go on to argue that such a chosen way of ending one's life should be made possible in a way that is humane, dignified, and serene. As it stands, that is rarely the case.

The Hemlock Society holds that, as in Holland, a physician aid-in-dying contract must be legalized in America so that the terminal, suffering patient can elect to have his dying accelerated in a dignified, failsafe way. Here the doctor is protected from criminal prosecution, the patient from prolonged suffering. No less important, close relatives are spared painful decision-making and risk-taking in helping a loved one die.

Until such a law is enacted, the old and infirm will have recourse only to whatever desperate measures are within their means: pills (will there be enough?), plastic bags, razor blades, knives or guns wielded by feeble hands. Also, the knowledge that, if a gun is used, there will be that terrible moment that will seem, ironically, like a lifetime, when someone must see and hear and feel the last gasps of the spouse he (or she) has just shot before turning the gun on himself.

There has to be a better way.

Appendix

Appendix A:

A Comparison of Mercy-killing Cases* and Simultaneous Deaths

A study of mercy-killing cases that have occurred in the last 67 years shows similar patterns to those of simultaneous deaths. Not surprisingly, aging, fragile health, and desperation are precipitating factors in the majority of instances. Also, there was a dramatic increase in the number of reported cases after 1980: Between 1920 and 1975, 31 incidents were officially recorded (none, apparently, between 1976 and 1979), whereas during the seven-year period after 1980, there were 67 documented cases. In the former (1920–75), there was only one suicide attempt. Here a man who had shot his severely handicapped adult daughter also shot himself. He survived the shooting and was acquitted of homicide on grounds of temporary insanity.

After 1980, of the 67 reported cases, one-quarter (17) of these were attempted double

---

*A mercy-killing case is defined here as one in which a person—a loved one (spouse, relative, caretaker, or close friend)—takes the life of someone who is catastrophically ill and who is usually dying. Often the aid in dying has been requested because the patient is incapable of acting on his or her own; sometimes it is unrequested, the life-taker electing to decide for them both.

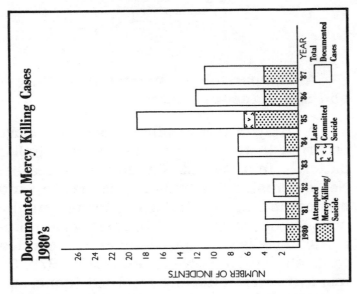

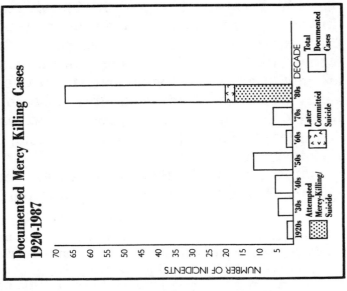

suicides, with all but two involving a husband who survived after taking the life of an ailing, elderly wife. In the other two, badly handicapped children were either shot or suffocated.

Before 1980

A closer look at the 30 cases recorded between 1920 and 1975 reveals that the majority of them (90%) occurred in the immediate family, although fewer spouses were involved than sons, daughters, siblings, or parents.

Where one spouse took the life of another, a lingering, life-threatening illness appeared to tax the emotional and physical resources of the caretaker/partner, leading to a desperate and violent death for the ailing husband or wife. Guns, strangulation, beating, stabbing, and electrocution were methods used, with prison terms for four of the nine surviving partners.

Surprisingly, courts showed greatest sympathy for parents who had taken the life of a son or daughter. Of nine cases, only one man received a prison sentence. The others were acquitted or released on probation. Typical of these were Louis Repouille and Herman Nagle. In 1939, after finding Repouille guilty of second-degree manslaughter for asphyxiating his 13-year-old "incurable imbecile" son, a judge suspended his sentence. However, the court warned the defendant that the law in no way sanctioned mercy killings and that "there is grave danger that the leniency extended to you may encourage others to do what you did."

In the case of Nagle, who shot his badly handicapped daughter in 1953, a jury acquitted him of first-degree murder after a highly emotional trial. When the verdict was announced, several observers stood and applauded.

Already the courts were in the delicate position of extending mercy to defendants who were clearly "guilty" of homicide, yet whose family circumstances elicited sympathy from judge and jury, a dilemma not easily or consistently resolved. Typically, when more brutal methods were used—one man electrocuted his mongoloid son—the court was not so merciful, in this case sentencing the defendant to death. The sentence was later commuted to life imprisonment and the defendant, himself a lawyer, eventually paroled.

In two highly publicized cases, one in 1950 and the other in 1972, two physicians injected terminally ill patients—one with air, the other with potassium chloride—in what courts later claimed were instances of murder. In New Hampshire in 1950, Dr. Hermann N. Sander was charged with first-degree murder after injecting Abbie Borroto, a patient in the final stages of cancer, with 40 cc's of air. A week later, Sander dictated his actions in the hospital record, noting that Borroto died minutes later; a librarian subsequently brought the report to the attention of the hospital administration and authorities.

During his trial, Sander claimed that Mrs. Borroto may have been dead when the injection was given. A jury apparently agreed by declaring Sander not guilty, a verdict received with gasps of joy by spectators.

Still, the issue of mercy killing was sidestepped, just as it was in the case of Vincent Montemarano, charged with willful murder after injecting a cancer-ridden patient with potassium chloride in 1972. Again, the defense claimed that the patient was already dead when Dr. Montemarano had examined him, never conceding that an injection had been administered. When the jury announced Montemarano not guilty, pandemonium broke out in the courtroom, once more underscoring the emotional nature of such trials.

However, little had been clarified or resolved in terms of mercy-killing cases and the law. That patients' dying and suffering were being increasingly prolonged by more sophisticated medical techniques was never tackled, leading to even more confusion when in the 1980s such cases, a quarter of which would be attempted double suicides, would increase at an alarming rate.

After 1980

With the ascendency of mercy killings came a slight shift in the patterning. First, while the majority of these occurred within the immediate family, significantly more took place between husbands and wives, with

Deceased's Relation to Instigator
(In Mercy Killings from 1920-1975)

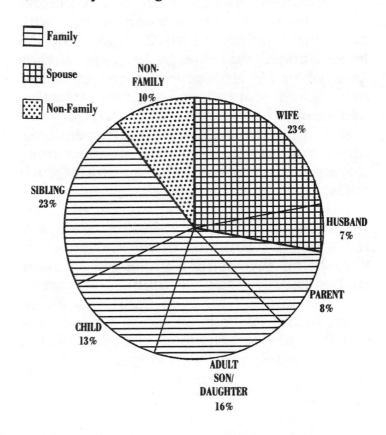

Deceased's Relation to Instigator
(In Mercy Killings from 1980-1987)

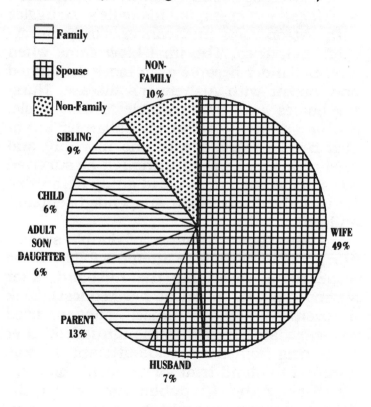

husbands more frequently taking a wife's life. Also, more grown children ended aged parents' lives.

When the husband ended his wife's life, in half the cases he also tried to kill himself but failed. Here, the wife's illness had become too distressing and prompted the final, desperate attempt to end it all. In Al Sallander's marriage, for example, his wife's struggles with osteoporosis and cancer slowly unravelled their lives. The final blow came when Mrs. Sallander became even more debilitated and violent with Alzheimer's disease. Nursing homes were unacceptable to the couple. As the situation worsened, Sallander strangled his 75-year-old wife one morning and slashed his own wrists, although he survived the suicide attempt to plead guilty to murder. He was given a five-year suspended sentence and probation.

A substantial number of double suicide or mercy killing/suicide attempts followed the same route. Invariably the husband, after slaying his wife (often at her request), took an overdose, stabbed himself, shot, or tried to asphyxiate himself—although failed. After recovering from the suicide attempt, he was required to stand trial for homicide or manslaughter. Although public support for the defendant was usually high, as one prosecutor commented, "It's against the law to take the life of someone else and we have to abide by the law whether we like it or not." Most defendants were acquitted or given a suspended sentence.

However, one man, 84-year-old Theodore Yankowich, after surviving a double suicide attempt by barbiturates, was convicted of manslaughter for his wife's death in 1985 and sentenced to 15 years house arrest. Arguing that Yankowich's suicide attempt occurred because of his "sense of wrongfulness" in helping his severely ill wife to die, prosecutors insisted on this type of penalty as a compromise between showing compassion for the defendant and punishing him.

A similar sentence was imposed on Bill Dixon in Fort Lauderdale, Florida. Dixon admitted shooting his 83-year-old wife who suffered from a long-term incurable illness. After pleading guilty to first-degree manslaughter, he was sentenced to nine years house arrest, like Yankowich. Despite the fact that both Mrs. Dixon and Mrs. Yankowich had been gravely ill for years and had repeatedly asked to be allowed to die, neither court regarded this as relevant. As one prosecutor said, "If you break the law, you must pay for it one way or another."

As a result, courts have been torn between making allowances for the defendant and setting an example for the public. Lacking a penal code which weighs the terminal condition of the deceased, considers whether death has been requested, and examines the motivation of the defendant (the case, for instance, in Switzerland and Germany), American courts must rely on a sympathetic judge and jury to wink at existing laws and defy them if they wish to behave humanely; after all, a life has been taken, the law broken. A more lenient outcome often depends on the rapport between the court and the person standing trial, leading to uneven and unpredictable results.

On the whole, defendants in mercy-killing cases have been treated with more clemency in the 1980s than in the previous six decades: Only 10% of those tried were imprisoned compared with 25% between 1920 and 1975. In the period between 1980 and 1985, two-thirds of the defendants received suspended sentences or probation. The remaining were either acquitted or not indicted. Usually leniency was displayed through reduced charges sanctioned by sympathetic prosecutors, judges, and juries. Contrite and grieving behavior on the part of the defendants invariably heightened sympathy, pointing to the poignancy of each case.

However, if the person on trial "performed" badly in court or had a particularly merciless prosecutor, the results could be harsher, leading to house arrest (as noted above) or imprisonment. These cases were a minority, but worth noting nonetheless. With Joseph Tynkody, one observer commented that he was prosecuted for having been trapped in the role of caretaker. For several years Tynkody had, with no outside help, cared for his severely afflicted 78-year-old wife, who also had Alzheimer's. Falls, disorientation, and pain exacerbated Mrs. Tynkody's confusion and discomfort, yet

Mercy Killing Cases
(1920-1985)

KEY

- Murder conviction / prison
- Manslaughter conviction / prison
- Manslaughter conviction / suspended sentence or probation
- Not Guilty / temporary insanity
- Acquittal
- Case dismissed
- Refusal to indict

1920's   1930's   1940's   1950's   1960's   1970's   1980–85

nursing homes were not considered a humane option by the couple. One evening, after a series of falls, Tynkody hurt his back trying to help her. Distraught and helpless, he shot his supine wife, afraid, as he later said, "If I had to go to the hospital, who was going to take care of her?"

The state claimed that the defendant's behavior was selfishly motivated. After Tynkody pleaded guilty to a reduced manslaughter charge and was given eight years in prison, the prosecutor said that he regretted the plea bargaining and had been too indulgent. "Our respect for life is just eroding," Thomas Sammon said. "If we ever have a euthanasia law in this country, it would be the downfall of our society."

Like charges were levelled at Roswell Gilbert in Florida in 1985 and John Forrest in 1987 in North Carolina. In the highly publicized trial of Gilbert, who, as mentioned earlier, shot his ailing wife twice in the head, a jury found him guilty of first-degree murder. Many observers speculated that Gilbert was a poor witness, showing no remorse or emotion while testifying, thus inviting a more severe penalty.

Similarly, after John Forrest shot his 83-year-old father in the head, the North Carolina Supreme Court upheld a life sentence for the defendant, who had been charged with first-degree murder. Ignoring the fact that Forrest Sn. had less than 24 hours to live and overlooking the prosecution's concession that the son's actions came from a desire not to have his father die a slow, painful death, the higher court stood firm: Evidence of deliberation and premeditation ruled out manslaughter charges, which included slayings through the "heat of passion." "We are unwilling to hold," Associate Justice Louis Meyer wrote for the Supreme Court, "that where the defendant kills a loved one in order to end the deceased's suffering, adequate provocation to negate malice is necessarily present." In other words, forethought, even if prompted by merciful considerations, is legally equated with malice and ill intent.

In three cases where parents ended the lives of children, two received probation while another was found guilty of first-degree murder. Once again, there was little uniformity in the processing of these cases. In Pennsylvania, Irene Bernstein shot her two and a half-year-old son, whose respiratory disorder affected the child's ability to walk and crawl. Apparently Mrs. Bernstein "snapped" under the stress of caring for her son. After pleading no contest to a third-degree murder charge, the court sentenced her to five years probation and 750 hours of community service. Esther Helton's shooting of her 46-year-old retarded daughter was similarly resolved in a Nevada County court in Arkansas.

Yet in Miami, Florida, a jury sentenced 25-year-old Charles Griffith to 25 years in prison for shooting his three-year-old daughter. A year earlier, the child had suffered irreversible brain damage when her head became wedged in the footrest of a reclining chair. She had lain comatose in a hospital since that time with no hope for recovery. Distraught by her condition, Griffith spent three final hours with his daughter before shooting her in the head. "All she knew was laughter and good times," he had said just before the shooting. "Now she just lies there. Just lies there."

At the trial, a jury rejected the defense's claim that Griffith was insane during the time of the shooting and found him guilty of murder. One juror later commented, "There was no verdict we felt could serve the law other than first degree. [Yet] the problem is that the law does not allow for what we thought this type of offense was."

Indeed, where the hopeless condition of the deceased has not been considered a mitigating factor, what choice is there when a life has been taken, whether a child's or an adult's? Judges and juries continue to grapple with these issues, straining a legal system that insists on technically disregarding circumstances surrounding death. In Walnut Creek, California, after an 84-year-old woman tried to end the life of her terminally ill husband by slashing his oxygen tubes, friends pointed out that Gilbert Bracken, 85, was dying slowly and painfully from emphysema and heart disease and had an agreement with his wife that neither would let the other suffer. "It was the disease killing him," one said. "The machines only prolonged his torment. It was his wife who tried to put him out of his misery."

In Houston in 1983, one physician argued that 62-year-old Robert Clore did not in fact die from the gunshot wound inflicted by Clore's 26-year-old son, who testified that he had been determined to end his father's suffering. Dr. Floyd Haas said that "There were so many other causes of death. His kidneys were very, very bad. He had pneumonia [and] his blood pressure had been extremely low." Nevertheless, a jury found Clore guilty of attempted murder, even though he received three years probation. Again, a sympathetic prosecutor did not recommend imprisonment. And, once again, the terminal condition of the deceased was ruled irrelevant.

"Plug-pulling" or passive euthanasia cases

As more of these cases are examined, burdens on family members tending the dying have become increasingly apparent, with little recourse in the courtroom for formal acknowledgment of this. Not only is the strain apparent when the patient has been cared for at home (usually by a sole caretaker, a spouse), more cases have surfaced in the 1980s where, like Gilbert Bracken's wife, a family member was indicted for homicide for removing the life supports of a loved one. In almost all cases, the patient had lost all or nearly all brain functioning, there was no hope for recovery, there was no Living Will or

Durable Power of Attorney for Health Care, and the hospital insisted on continuing treatment despite some family members' protestations.

Eventually one of them becomes desperate, later testifying to the futility and indignity of such artificial devices, and either removes tubes or holds the medical staff at bay while threatening to remove life supports. In six of the eight cases that have occurred, the defendant was released on probation after standing trial for murder, attempted murder or manslaughter.

In separate cases, two men held the medical staff at gunpoint while demanding that a loved one be disconnected from life-sustaining equipment. In Phoenix, Arizona, in 1986, 19-year-old Robert Whipple, described as "highly distraught," pointed a shotgun at doctors and nurses while demanding that they cut off the respirator and intravenous system keeping his 28-year-old brother alive. After he surrendered, Whipple (whose brother later died) was charged with attempted murder, kidnapping, and assault. He received five years probation.

In Martinez, California, Edward Baker was sentenced to three years probation after pleading guilty to manslaughter and assault with a deadly weapon. Baker, 38, had held a gun to the neck of a nurse tending his dying father, demanding that life-support machines be unplugged. The nurse did so and several minutes later Baker Sn., in the final throes of cancer of the esophagus, died. Later Baker testified that he had had a verbal agreement with his father dating back to his teens: "He made me promise not to let his life be maintained past a reasonable length of time by artificial means should the occasion ever arise."

Nurses and doctors have also been vulnerable to the strains of keeping long-suffering terminal patients alive, often against the patients' will. Compared with the three cases before 1975 (1925, 1950, and 1972), after 1980 there were eight instances where a physician or nurse ended the life of a gravely ill patient: six through injection and two by removing life supports. All except one were required to stand trial for homicide (three for first-degree murder).

The exception took place in Fairport, Connecticut, where 76-year-old Dr. John Kraii committed suicide while awaiting trial for the alleged murder of longtime patient and friend Frederick C. Wagner, 81. Kraii, apparently "overwhelmed" by Wagner's suffering, injected him with a lethal dose of insulin. A suicide note indicated that Kraii was disturbed by his failing health and by the thought of being prosecuted for homicide. At the time of Wagner's death, Roswell Gilbert was in the midst of his highly-publicized trial for the murder of his wife.

In the six instances where a doctor or nurse injected a terminally ill patient with a lethal dose or withheld medication, five defendants (one physician, four nurses) were put on probation or received suspended sentences. In each case medical licenses were temporarily revoked until the trial's end.

In Mays Landing, New Jersey, 51-year-old Joseph Hassman was fined $10,000 and ordered to perform 400 hours of community service for injecting his mother-in-law, Esther Davis, with lethal doses of Demerol and Visiral. Mrs. Davis, who had been confined to a convalescent center for years, had Alzheimer's disease and was in poor health.

And in Winston-Salem, North Carolina, the exception occurred: nurse Anthony Shook was convicted of first-degree murder and sentenced to life imprisonment in the killing of 35-year-old Peggy Lou Epley, hospitalized in a "chronic vegetative state" and not expected to survive. Shook had ended Epley's life by purposely withholding vital blood-pressure medication. Although Shook's guilt was never in question, one juror commented that many of them agreed that Epley's suffering was being endlessly prolonged. Yet, as he explained, "the real problem we had is that we felt he committed this act as an act of mercy toward the patient, and we had a hard time understanding why the penalty had to be so harsh when he did not have any gain for himself."

Methods

When comparing methods used in the 1980s with those used earlier, injections and withdrawal of life supports ("plug-pulling")

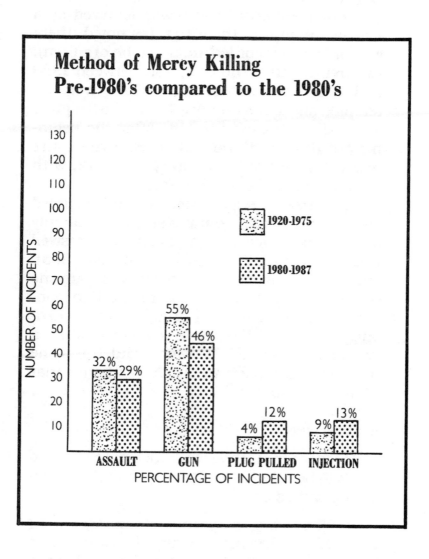

**Method of Mercy Killing
Pre-1980's compared to the 1980's**

increased slightly, while assault (asphyxiation, beating, knifing, electrocution) decreased.

When a mercy killing was followed by a suicide attempt in the 1980s (as noted, there was only one recorded instance before then), two trends can be noted: First, between 1980 and 1984, four out of 25, or 16%, were attempted simultaneous deaths, half with guns and half with asphyxiation. After the beginning of 1985 until the end of 1987, the figure rose to one out of three, or 14 out of 42, with guns the most frequently used method.

The rise in such cases in 1985 coupled with more suicide attempts suggests not only a "copy-cat" syndrome following Roswell Gilbert's shooting of his wife (March 1985), but also a sense of helplessness when anyone contemplating a mercy killing had to consider Gilbert's trial and guilty verdict. Obviously one would have to consider what a defendant observed: "I was afraid the same thing would happen to me. It was better that I kill myself too."

An overview

Figures from these recorded cases are too small to be considered final, although the following trends can be observed:

• While the majority of mercy-killing cases (90%) remain within the immediate family, in the last half-decade, over half have occurred between husbands and wives, and the number continues to climb dramatically.

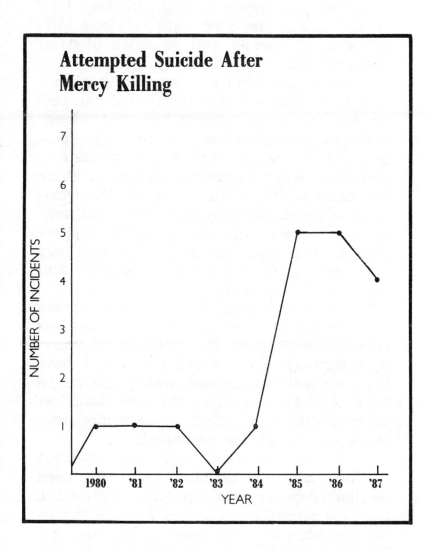

Attempted Suicide After Mercy Killing

NUMBER OF INCIDENTS

YEAR

In turn, most of these involve the husband taking the life of his spouse. One quarter of the time, the husband attempted suicide following the mercy killing. In one fifth of the cases, the wife suffered from Alzheimer's disease as well as other physical complications.

• Fewer defendants in mercy-killing cases have been imprisoned in the 1980s than previously. In general, courts have a tendency to show greater clemency through plea-bargaining, community service, probation, and suspended sentences, although there has been a lack of uniformity in the treatment of those standing trial. Evidence indicates that pre-trial publicity and the rapport between the defendant and judge and jury can gratuitously affect the assessment and outcome of each case.

• The percentage of doctors and nurses in mercy-killing cases involving a patient has remained consistent over the last 65 years: Approximately 10% of those indicted have been medical staff. To date, nearly all charges have been dismissed, or the defendant has been acquitted, received a suspended sentence, or been put on probation.

• As is the case with simultaneous deaths, guns are the most frequently used method; they are used approximately half the time. In recent years, mercy killings involving injection or withdrawal of life supports have increased from just over 10% to one-quarter.

As distressing as the increase in all these cases is, equally distressing is the courts' inability to deal consistently and fairly with defendants who have helped a loved one to die. In most cases, juries have chosen to reinterpret the law; regardless of instructions to disregard a defendant's motives, where leniency is shown the jury has obviously queried underlying causes of the defendant's conduct. If the person on trial, like Roswell Gilbert, shows little remorse or emotion, judgment will be more severe.

However, when circumstances surrounding the mercy killing provoke sympathy, motive is obliquely considered through alternative, often devious ploys: Temporary insanity pleas, often patently contrived, are offered, and lesser degrees of homicide are sanctioned, despite the deliberate (albeit compassionate) taking of another's life. These are fictions that do little to enhance court proceedings and are, in fact, abuses of the law.

Nothing will improve until three factors are considered: the terminal condition of the deceased, whether death was requested, and how humanely the defendant was motivated in taking a loved one's life.

Until courts weigh these as relevant issues in determining the guilt or innocence of the person on trial, inconsistent and unfair results will continue. Also, many involved in mercy-killing cases will consider suicide inescapable knowing that a zealous prosecutor, such as Gilbert's, might rule out any mitigating circumstances. A trial for murder, emotionally harrowing and costly, is too overwhelming for some who are already devastated by their loss.

The most sensible and humane alternative appears to be to adapt the Swiss and German method, in which a special statutory provision in the penal code recognizes mercy killing as a separate crime. Here, different criteria than those used in homicide cases are applied. As has been demonstrated in these two countries, a mercy-killing case can be properly assessed in a law court without straining the credulity and imaginative resources of judge, jury, prosecuting and defense attorneys.

So, too, such a change would confirm what is apparent in so many of these cases: that the taking of another's life, while not permissible in the eyes of the law, can still be a loving and compassionate act.

end

About the author:

Ann Wickett, co-founder and deputy director of the National Hemlock Society, is co-author of *Jean's Way* and *The Right to Die*. In the last eight years, she has been the editor of the Hemlock Quarterly and the Euthanasia Review. She lives on a farm in Western Oregon.

Other books from The Hemlock Society

The Right to Die: Understanding Euthanasia
By Derek Humphry and Ann Wickett

An in-depth overview of the historical, cultural, social and psychological aspects of euthanasia.

Harper and Row
$9.95 paperback   New York

Euthanasia and Religion: A Survey of the Attitudes of World Religions to the Right-To-Die
By Gerald A. Larue

$10.00   Distributed by Grove Press
New York

Commonsense Suicide: The Final Right
By Doris Portwood

An honest examination of the last taboo in our society.

$8   Distributed by Grove Press
                                      New York

Jean's Way
By Derek Humphry with Ann Wickett

The true story of one woman's plans to end her own life towards the end of a terminal illness. The book is helpful to other couples in a similar predicament. 1986 edition

$6.95   Harper and Row
                                      New York

Compassionate Crimes, Broken Taboos

A compilation of famous euthanasia cases from around the world. Invaluable as source material for researchers. Updated 1986.

$5 (includes mailing)   The Hemlock Society

All the above books can be purchased by mail order from Hemlock, PO Box 11830, Eugene OR 97440. Please add $2 for shipping and handling.

As part of its purpose to educate the public on issues of voluntary euthanasia, the National Hemlock Society publishes books and a journal on euthanasia and related subjects. Formed in Los Angeles, California, in 1980, the nonprofit, tax-deductible organization now operates from Eugene, Oregon. The annual membership fee is $20, which can include a couple. Over 60's: $15 annually.

For further details, write:
The National Hemlock Society
PO Box 11830
EUGENE OR 97440–3900

Telephone: 503/342–5748